A Year Underwater

Twelve Months of Diving, Fraternizing with Marine Life, and Just Having a Great Time, from the St. Lawrence River to West Palm Beach

Jerry Shine

Blue Sphere Pubs
www.bluesphere.us

Published by Blue Sphere Pubs
www.bluesphere.us

First printing 2017

ISBN 978-0-9988901-0-4
Library of Congress Number 2017905231
Manufactured in the United States

WARNING

Diving is a potentially dangerous activity that can result in serious injury or death. This book is not a substitute for professional scuba instruction. It is not a guide to any of the dive sites included within, and in no way describes all of the potential dangers that could be encountered at any of these sites. It is also not an endorsement of or recommendation for diving or snorkeling alone.

Also by Jerry Shine

A Shore Diving Guide to New England

Nudibranchs of the Northeast

We need a whole new vocabulary, new adjectives, adequately to describe the designs and colors of under sea.

William Beebe

To my son, Zeke.
Hold on to what you love, buddy.

A Year Underwater

The sun had come up but still hung low over the homes on Bearskin Neck, the spit of land jutting out into the Atlantic across the bay in Rockport, Massachusetts. I walked up the concrete ramp from the beach, leaving a trail of watery footprints to my car, and set down my tank. As I did, a pair of joggers rounded the corner, exhalations trailing behind them in the cold air.

They slowed to a stop. On what should have been an empty street on New Year's morning, cars were parked from one end to the other. White smoke from barbecues rose up between them, while crowds of people milled about in various stages of undress. The pair then looked at me and the puddle forming around my feet.

"Happy New Year," I said.

The two looked at each other and burst out laughing.

"Did you just come out of the ocean?" the woman asked.

"I did."

She stared at me, flabbergasted. "How cold is the water?"

"It's about forty degrees."

"Forty degrees!"

"That's actually not bad," I said.

"Not bad!"

Clearly, she was a repeater.

"What do you consider bad?" she asked.

"Well, when it gets down into the mid-thirties, that's when you start to feel it."

"The mid-thirties!" She raised her hands as if to grab me by the chest and shake me. She didn't though. "That suit keeps you warm?"

"It does," I said. "I was just in for an hour."

"That's crazy," her partner said, shaking his head.

"And all of these people," she motioned up the street, "they were diving, too?"

I looked over my shoulder. About 20 people were gearing up, with another 20 helping. "I don't think any of them have been in yet but they will be soon. It's a good way to start off the year."

She turned to her friend. "And people think we're crazy for *running* in the winter."

He laughed and nodded and she looked back at me. She seemed at a loss for words. "Well," she finally said, "Happy New Year."

They broke back into their jog. But while the man stared at the divers they were about to run through, the woman looked to her left, out over the beach and the blue water just beyond.

She stopped and turned back to me. "So what did you see down there?"

A seagull overhead let out a shriek as it flew off with a piece of barbecue. So what did I see down there? A little backstory first. I bought my first dive mask when I was five years old. I put two quarters down on the counter of the boathouse on Lake Mamanasco and was given a box with a white plastic mask inside. My life hasn't been the same since. I don't really remember what happened in the next few minutes but the odds are good that I put on the mask, walked into the lake, stuck my head underwater, and when I came up, someone on the beach yelled, "So what did you see down there?"

Back in Rockport, a scrum of cawing seagulls gave chase to the one with the barbecue.

So what did I see down there?

In all the years I've been diving, as I've stood by the water gearing up or gearing down, I've probably been asked that question a thousand times.

And the answer should be easy. There's nowhere in the world you can get closer to wildlife than you can underwater. But how do you tell someone about the seal that appeared out of nowhere to play with your fins, or the giant mola mola lolling about on the surface, or the massive school of pollock that swirled around you, all within a stone's throw of the beach? How do you tell someone how it *feels* to be surrounded by the ocean and the life within it?

You can't. There isn't enough time.

So instead of answering, I'm left saying things like, "Oh, it's amazing down there," or, "It's pretty incredible."

If there's a child in tow, there might be a follow-up question, usually about sharks or sea turtles. One little girl asked if I had ever seen a nudibranch. That one impressed me. I try to answer these more conscientiously. But even then, there's usually a parent with places to go, people to see, pulling the child in the opposite direction.

My point is that in all of those times that I've been asked what I see down there, never have I had the chance to truly answer. Not once.

Until now.

Winter

I left my home in Somerville, Massachusetts at four o'clock the next morning and drove north through roads that grew ever narrower and less populated, all the way to Eastport, Maine – about as far up the Maine coast as you can go before hitting Canada.

As long drives go, it was an easy one, with little traffic. As I drove, though, I wished I'd been able to postpone. The week before, the weather reports had looked fine. Then two friends, Ed Monat from Bar Harbor, Maine and Joe George from New Brunswick, decided to come along, too. I should have known then that things were going to go bad.

Joe's nickname is Stormbringer. And it's an apt one. Wherever he goes, howling winds and crashing waves seem to follow.

There were still no storms predicted but forecasts were now calling for bitterly cold air temperatures. If it had just been me, I would have postponed. But with Ed and Joe on the way, I couldn't.

So north I went. And six hours later, I pulled onto

Eastport's main road.

In the dead of winter, Eastport, the easternmost city in the U.S., seems a lonely place. The main street was almost completely devoid of traffic. Most of the storefronts along it were either vacant or closed. And I could count on one hand the number of people who were out and about. It was hard to believe that much of anything ever happened here. But it did.

Through Eastport's early years, a seemingly endless supply of herring fed a string of canneries that jammed the waterfront, employing thousands. Ships built here were spread out over the world's oceans. Even as late as World War II, there were crowds, theaters, energy.

No more, though. The herring are gone, and with them, the canneries. The city's population is now less than a third of what it was in its heyday.

Eastport is one of my favorite places in the world, though. There's more to it than meets the eye – and a fair amount of that is underwater.

Just past the empty storefronts, a brick building sat crumbling under its own weight – one last vestige of the old cannery industry. The pillars supporting it from underneath were disintegrating, their middles wasting away like so many load-bearing hourglasses. A few years earlier, there had been a plan afoot to renovate it into 'luxury condos' overlooking the bay, but even the sign announcing it had taken on an abandoned look.

Beyond the building, the paved road turned to

dirt and then the waterfront opened up, unobstructed.

"Woo-hoo!" Joe yelled, standing on a rattan mat in the snow, wearing nothing but his boxer shorts and a watch cap.

"Woo-hoo!" Ed yelled from the back of his pick-up truck, parked on the other side of the road. Huge stickers of underwater superheroes in battle poses adorned the truck. His dark, shaggy hair was pulled back in a loose ponytail.

As soon as I got out of my car, Ed was there, already in his drysuit, and he pulled me into a bear hug.

"Oh, my God," he yelled – Ed pretty much always yells – "you wouldn't believe how long it took us to get here!"

His wife Edna waved from the cab of their pick-up.

"We had to stop to get a part for the boat, then I had to get more carabiners for my camera ..."

In what had been the quiet of a winter day in Eastport, Ed's voice was now reverberating off the side of the old cannery and out over the bay.

"... and then we had to stop to see a guy about a salvage job. It's taken us, like, 24 hours to get here!"

"Plus you had to stop to have sex," Joe yelled.

"Yeah, but that was only two minutes," Ed yelled back.

"Two minutes?"

"Okay, one minute."

"Yeah, maybe it was just a rolling stop," Joe yelled. His voice was now reverberating off the side of the cannery, too.

Ed, a.k.a., Diver Ed, runs the Dive-In Theater with Edna from their boat, the *Starfish Enterprise*, in Bar Harbor.

Throughout the summer, they take passengers out to the bay. Ed then dives, transmitting a live video and audio feed back to the boat, which is set up like an outdoor theater. It's the next best thing to being underwater.

Kids, in particular, love him. If there's any way for him to show them the butthole of a creature he's filming, he will. If he catches it in the act of actually pooping, so much the better. Instead of a buddy, he brings a tiny action figure, Mini Ed, underwater with him. Mini Ed just wants to love all the creatures they find but he's constantly under attack from lobsters and crabs.

At the end of each dive, Ed has the kids onboard overinflate his neoprene suit until he's blown up like the Michelin Man. The number of people who've walked off his boat thrilled about the ocean, excited about marine life and wanting to learn more, now reaches up into the thousands.

Joe, on the other hand, started out adult life in the Canadian military. After being discharged, he worked as a commercial diver on oil rigs in the Gulf of Mexico. When that dried up, he went back into the Canadian Army, where he still is, as a combat diver and a dive supervisor.

Joe stepped out from behind his van to give me a hug. He was in his drysuit, too, ready to go.

Ed pulled on his tank. As he did, I could hear him singing a soft, crooning ballad to himself.

> *I'm going diving with Jerry Shine,*
> *the pleasure will be all mine.*
> *It will be such a wonderful time,*
> *underwater with Jerry Shine.*

The view from the road of what's left of the old pier, looking out over the intertidal zone, the stumps of old pilings and the top of the footing. The footing drops straight down underwater, with only its offshore side exposed.

The song then looped back around and repeated. Ed sings these whenever we dive together. The songs are always different but always about me. I'm not sure he even realizes he's doing it.

With his tank on, Ed started down to the water still singing, Joe behind him. I knew neither of them were going to wait so I hustled to gear up as quickly as possible. I pulled on my thermals and drysuit, attached my regulator and BC to my tank, strapped on my weight belt, hooked my camera to the D-rings on my tank's chest straps (it's too heavy to carry easily), and grabbed my mask and fins.

The air temperature was 28 degrees – the warmest it was going to be for a while.

The tide was out and the water, which laps right up to the side of the road at high tide, was now a good 50 yards away, out past the mud and gravel and seaweed of the intertidal zone. Dozens of old pilings rose up from the mud like so many tree stumps – the last remains of a long-gone pier. The only other remnant was the pier's footing, all the way down at the water's edge. The top of it broke the surface, a jumble of massive granite blocks covered in rockweed. All around it, eddies swirled and churned. I could actually hear the water moving – not in waves toward the beach but in tidal flow parallel to it.

This is the Bay of Fundy, where the most powerful tides in the world surge in and out twice a day – 160 billion tons of seawater in a state of near-perpetual movement. The only time you can dive here without being swept away is at slack water – that hour or so in between the tides, when the water slows and stops before turning and heading back the other way.

Joe and Ed were already in so I finished gearing up and picked my way over the rip rap at the side of the road and then down the intertidal. As I did, a sudden gust of wind whipped up a flurry of snow and sent it swirling around me.

At the near end of the old footing, I walked into the water, pulled on my fins and headed under.

The press of the water and its thick silence feels wonderful. The slope of the bottom is immediate – a sharp, sandy drop-off. What's left of the ebbing current is pulling sand off the bottom and sending it up into the water column around me. But a couple of quick kicks and I'm down the slope into deeper water. The current eases, the sand clears, and visibility opens to a murky ten feet.

The corner of the footing is directly to my right. Underwater, it looks nothing like it does on the surface. Granite blocks, about four feet by six feet, are stacked neatly on top of and beside one another, forming a flat wall set right into the slope, with only its offshore side exposed. The wall rises straight up from the bottom all the way to the surface, some 35 feet above. Cracks and crevices form everywhere between the blocks. Most are narrow. Some are large enough to peer into.

For as far as I can see, which isn't far, life and color – frilled anemones, northern red anemones, yellow sponges, flat tunicates, starfish – are splashed across the wall like a Jackson Pollock come to life. Groups of sea peaches – orange spheres the size of lacrosse balls, with siphons visibly sucking water in, filtering it for food and blowing it back out, are all over. So are stalked tunicates – animals similar to the sea peaches but with foot-long stems for them to feed farther out from the wall.

Ledges form everywhere a block extends beyond the one above. A beautifully ugly sculpin watches me from one. I drift in close and, as I do, it spreads its large pectoral fins, rises from the ledge and glides down into the gloom.

I put a finger on the ledge and peer into a crevice. A crab inside, startled, raises its claws, then scurries deeper in.

Most of the anemones on the wall are northern reds. Despite their name, only some are red. Others are orange. Some are purple. A few are white. Most are open, with thick, finger-like tentacles reaching out in search of prey. Down here, countless animals look like plants but anemones may be the extreme.

I stop in front of a trio of them, each close to a foot in diameter. The block they're attached to has a series of cuts on its lower edge, making it easy to find and recognize, which I've been doing since my first dive here some 20 years ago. In all that time, these three anemones haven't moved more than a few inches, even though they're more than capable. But with the tides constantly pulling so much food through, there's no need.

As I watch, a green urchin comes tumbling down from above in slow motion. A second urchin does the same, a few feet to the left. Then a third. I can hear the engine of a fishing boat chugging in the distance, and the waves from its wake must be hitting the top of the wall hard enough to dislodge the urchins.

A fourth tumbles down but lands on the outstretched tentacles of one of the anemones. In an instant, the tentacles close over it. On a scale too small to see, hundreds of thin membranes on the tentacles have just flown open, releasing explosive, harpoon-like nematocysts coiled within. The nematocysts are barbed, armed with poison that can kill or paralyze, and connected back to the anemone by thin filaments. Right now, a circular muscle at the base of the tentacles is retracting like a drawstring, pulling the tentacles in, drawing the urchin straight into the anemone's mouth at their center.

In seconds, the urchin is gone. I can still see the shape of its spiny body pushing out through the anemone's side. How the anemone can withstand its sharp spines is beyond me. Digestion of it might take weeks and any by-products will have to be defecated back out through the anemone's mouth, which doubles as its anus. So much for intelligent design.

I drift down all the way to the base of the wall. The bottom is a mix of gravel and rocky ledge pushing up through it. There's junk everywhere: pieces of big PVC pipe, sheets of scrap metal and rusted engine parts. Massive timbers are also strewn about – more remnants of the old pier. Some crisscross like giant Lincoln Logs. Some sit parallel to one another. A few are off by themselves. Like the wall, most teem with life. Others are oddly barren.

I kneel down in front of one. A hermit crab on top of it panics and charges straight off into the water column. For a moment, it hangs there cartoon-like, its legs windmilling wildly, then drops to the bottom and rushes off.

I scoot sideways along the timber's length. A large shrimp clinging to its side flicks off and disappears. A rock gunnel – a small, eel-like fish – swishes into a clump of stalked tunicates and turns back to stare out at me. A pair of reddish brown sea raven – fish whose bodies are decorated with seaweed-like tabs that dangle off them for camouflage – sit side-by-side on the timber, refusing to move.

Out in the gloom, offshore from the wall, a pair of bright lights, like the headlights of a pickup truck, are coming up the slope. It's Ed shooting video. In another moment, the lights swing to the side and disappear.

I swim away from the wall and the bottom turns to gravel and mud. A pair of basket stars – starfish with long, branching, tendril-like arms – sit on the bottom, each holding onto a separate rock, reaching up into the water column to catch food.

Glass bottles are everywhere, thrown from the pier and the boats that tied up to it 100, 200 years ago. Most are broken but a few are intact. Every winter, storms unearth a whole new cache of them from the mud.

I'm 60 feet deep and a school of about 200 pollock – green, sleek and built for speed – swims just overhead, swirling above like a river. I rise up and try to get close but they speed up and swim off.

I drift back down to the bottom. The gravel and mud is so nondescript here, and the slope away from the shoreline so slight, that it's impossible to know which way I'm heading. I check my compass and take a bearing back to the wall. I start in that direction and come face-to-face with a monster lobster – it looks to weigh 20 pounds. It's the biggest one I've ever seen. Barnacles cover its shell. Its claws look too heavy to lift. It isn't moving and for a second I wonder if it's dead. But then the smaller of its two pairs of antennae begin waving back and forth, searching the water for chemical traces of predators or prey.

Most lobsters have already moved offshore until spring. But this one is big enough to ride out whatever the New England winter has in store for it. It's so big that I want someone else to see it. I look for Ed's lights but he's gone. Joe is nowhere to be seen either. It's just this monster lobster and me, face-to-face, alone in the murk.

"So we'll meet at Dawsons tomorrow at the same time," Ed said, his voice high, almost yelling.

"Woo-hoo!" Joe said, almost yelling, too.

I wasn't feeling the 'woo-hoo' though. I wanted to hang with these guys but we weren't even dry and Joe was already heading back to Canada. And Ed and Edna had checked into a different motel than I had.

After the early start, though, the long drive, and the hour in cold water, what I needed was to hunker down with some take-out and a Bruins game. As for hanging out – well, tomorrow. I drove 45 minutes to my motel, checked in and fell asleep.

When I woke up two hours later, it was already dark. I stepped out to find a restaurant and immediately felt the difference: the air temperature had dropped about 20 degrees. I popped the trunk of my car and shined a light inside. All of my gear was frozen solid. I made a mental note to bring it into the room with me when I got back.

Early the next morning, I pulled aside the drapes in my room and looked out at the parking lot. Harsh sunlight glared off the iced-over windows and windshields of every car in it. Two big tractor-trailer trucks were warming up, their engines rumbling while the whitest of smoke billowed from their exhausts. A chambermaid, bundled up from head to toe with only her eyes visible, hurried by clutching an armful of blankets.

It was five degrees outside.

To dive in weather like this must seem crazy. And

it probably is. But not to the extent you might think. Winter diving is like skiing: you know it's going to be cold and you dress for it. Rather than wearing a wetsuit that lets in a bit of water and can only keep you so warm, you wear a drysuit that lets in none, with a set of heavy thermals underneath.

I had time to kill before I had to get to the site so I stayed in the room, working, reading, checking the weather. A storm that was supposed to swing out to sea was now going to hit late in the afternoon. Joe George had struck again. What's more, he e-mailed that his wife Connie wasn't feeling well and he wouldn't even be coming today.

I looked out at the parking lot again. The cold was so pervasive that I could *see* it. I put on my drysuit in the room so I wouldn't have to change outside.

I parked at Dawson Street, a few hundred yards down the road from where we had dived yesterday. A thick blanket of Arctic-like sea smoke hung over the water. A pair of fishing boats pulled away from the dock just up the channel and were quickly swallowed up in it.

To reach the water here, you have to walk through someone's side yard, which always feels funny to me. I haven't cut through someone's yard since I was 15. But this is actually a public right-of-way, although no signs mark it as such.

A half-hour later, slack water was getting close and Ed and Edna still weren't there. I was about to call him when he called me.

"Man, we're not even in Eastport anymore," he yelled. "Our neighbor called us last night. There was something was wrong with our dogs. They wouldn't stop barking so we had to come home!"

As it turned out, their dogs, a pair of massive Newfoundlands, were fine.

I, on the other hand, was now alone in an Arctic vortex I hadn't wanted to come to in the first place. I was tempted to just blow off the dive and head home. But as I stared at the water, a question that's tugged at me for as long as I can remember, tugged at me again: what's happening under there right now?

I geared up and made my way across the frozen lawn. The air temperature had climbed to 17 degrees.

Cut, jagged rocks encrusted with a hard, pink coral carpet the shallows. The slope is gentle at first but then drops down sharply, split by a pair of dark, vertical ledges that push straight out from it side-by-side. Both are so covered with life that it's almost impossible to see any of the rock beneath. Stalked tunicates are vibrating in the current like dozens of tulips blowing in the wind. Yellow sponges, soft red corals and anemones are squeezed between them. The ledges aren't just alive with color but movement. Rock crabs, green crabs and hermit crabs are moving up and down, on top of the attached invertebrates.

I move past the two ledges to a smaller one that juts out from the bottom like a rounded boulder. There's almost no life on it. I drift in close to a dark opening near the top and a blue face and head, the size of a cantaloupe, looms up from inside. The face is lined with white scars and its sharp, canine-like teeth are fully exposed. As ugly as it is – and it is ugly – the face is almost human, which may be the scariest part.

It's a wolffish and, despite its looks, it isn't dangerous at all. It's Gene – so named by Jonathan Bird of PBS's *Jonathan Bird's Blue World*. Jonathan owns a house across the street and met Gene on a dive here 20 years ago. Since then, Gene has been introduced to dozens of other divers. Many hand-feed him urchins and he now comes out when he sees us coming. He even has his own Facebook page.

He isn't coming out today, though. He stares at me from the hole, mouth opening and closing as he breathes. It's possible he recognizes me as the guy who never feeds him. The Buddhist in me won't allow it.

But even from his hole, it's obvious what a spectacular piece of evolution he is. His exposed canines are just the start of his dental work. Deeper in, the roof of his mouth is lined with crushing teeth that pulverize urchins and grind up heavy clam shells. His lower jaw also has several rows of molars, with even more teeth deeper down his throat, just in case.

And all of these teeth get replaced every year. When the new ones come in, they'll take up to three months to harden, during which time he'll eat nothing. We stare at each other for a few minutes until he loses interest and pulls into his hole, disappearing into the dark.

I hadn't been cold underwater but back on the beach my hair was frozen and my fingers were stinging. I pulled off my gear as fast as I could while a woman walking a pair of black labs passed by.

The dogs paid no attention to me but when they stopped to sniff in the bushes beside my car, the woman – bundled up and dragging on a cigarette – gave my gear a sidelong glance.

"Well, it's not for me to judge," she deadpanned, her Maine accent thick, "but I have a feeling you're crazy."

I laughed, still pulling off my drysuit. The dogs were now shoulder-deep in the shrubbery and didn't look like they'd be moving anytime soon.

She gave the leashes a couple of tugs then looked back at me and shrugged. "I don't see anyone with you," she finally said.

"My friends all chickened out," I laughed. The truth is I've been making easy shore dives like this by myself for decades.

The woman nodded. And the dogs were ready to move on.

I got in my car and started the long drive home, congratulating myself for getting out before the storm hit. Thirty minutes later, though, the first snowflakes began to fall, fat and fast. There was almost no traffic but what little there was, was in a hurry. Timber trucks loaded down with massive tree trunks barreled by. I prayed as I fishtailed on each icy uphill. I prayed even harder sliding on each icy downhill, particularly the sharp turns right in the middle of them.

Four hours of white-knuckle driving later, the storm petered out and I was able to loosen my grip on the steering wheel.

****

A week later, I parked in front of the Aquatic Center in Danvers, Massachusetts. The Arctic cold had broken and the January afternoon felt like a spring day. A few minutes later, Bobby Boyle pulled in and parked beside me.

He leaned out his window and waved, then closed his eyes and angled his face up to the sun. His whitish-blonde hair was close-cropped, his hairline starting to recede.

I first met Bob when I signed up for his underwater photography class a year or two after I was certified to dive. I walked in knowing nothing about cameras, lenses or f-stops. By the time it was over, I actually had some publishable shots. He was a good teacher.

He was also a local celebrity. Everybody knew him. Everybody liked him. Newspapers regularly called him for underwater photos or quotes about diving or to run profiles on him.

He made a dive every morning before going into work at his dive shop and that's where we started to become friends. I'd get to a site early, thinking I'd be the first one there, and he'd be coming out of the water as I'd be going in. He always wanted to know where I had been diving, what I had been shooting, what I had been shooting with. And I have to admit that I enjoyed these brushes with celebrity, especially if I had a girlfriend on hand.

At some point, though, I started running into him less and less. Eventually, I stopped seeing him altogether.

"All right," he said, opening his door, "let's do this."

I pushed his wheelchair up to the side of his SUV and locked it in place.

"Beautiful," he said, scooting in. "I'm ready."

When Bob was in his forties, he started falling for no apparent reason. Sometimes he found himself without the strength to do simple things. His neck grew distended. His voice became higher and flatter. If someone took a photo of him, he could feel the electricity of the flash moving through him. He could still dive but only on good days. And at some point, even the good days weren't good enough.

Doctors were baffled but he was finally diagnosed with Mitochondrial Epilepsy with Ragged Red Fibers – MERRF – a rare, progressive, degenerative disease with no known cure. He was one of the few adults in the world who had it (it mainly affects children) and his doctors had no answers for the symptoms he was experiencing. They were learning more from him than he was from them.

Over time, he went from using a cane, to using forearm crutches, to short stints in a wheelchair, to being wheelchair-bound. Even breathing could be difficult and pneumonia would send him to the hospital for long stays. Each time he went in, he seemed to degenerate so much and so fast that it was hard to imagine him coming back out and being able to live independently. But each time he would somehow bounce back – though never quite to the level he had been at before going in.

He still ran his shop. He still chartered boats to take others out. He still drove loops around Gloucester and Rockport every morning on his way into work to check conditions and report them to divers. And he still went to Bonaire – an island in the Caribbean – a couple of times a year. He was hoping to go again in a few months and perhaps even dive. It was easier there. The water was warmer, the wetsuits were thinner and the weight belts were lighter. But he needed to know if his lungs still functioned well enough to breathe through a regulator underwater.

It was a weekday afternoon and we had the place to ourselves. There was no one in either of the two pools. I wheeled Bob up to a ladder in the deep end of one and started sorting through his gear.

As always, I wasn't sure how much help to give him: how hard to pull on his fins; how much to work my fingers inside his mask to make it seal; how much lift to give him out of the chair and to the edge of the pool. I didn't want him to work harder than he could but I didn't want to embarrass him either.

Bob just laughed. "Beautiful," he said at each step along the way.

And then he was in the water, free from gravity. He took a moment to catch his breath, then told me he was going to try to swim the length of the pool and back underwater. With a smile, he put the regulator in his mouth, deflated his BC and dropped under.

On the bottom, he adjusted his gear, then started kicking slowly, his arms moving in small breaststroke motions. I swam above him on the surface. He reached the wall, made a wide loop and headed back. Without coming up, he swam a second lap, moving more confidently.

When he made it back to the ladder, he came up, pumped some air into his BC to float, then leaned back and closed his eyes with a smile. "Oh, yeah."

"No problems?"

"None," he said.

"You want to go back under?"

He seemed tired but not ready to get out. "One more lap." He let the air out of his BC, dropped to the bottom and started to kick again.

As we reached the wall and turned around, a woman came out of the locker room onto the pool deck. She tried to squeeze past Bob's wheelchair to get to the ladder. When she couldn't, she moved it aside, climbed halfway down and began exercising, pulling herself up and down on the ladder's handrails.

"Excuse me," I called, "would you mind using a different ladder?" Between the two pools, there were seven others.

She stared at me blankly.

I pointed at Bob's wheelchair. "We're coming out there."

She looked up at the wheelchair as if somehow seeing it for the first time, then back at me. "I'm only going to be five minutes," she said sternly. "And I don't like stopping once I've started." She went back to her pull-ups.

Over the years, I had heard Bob talk about people who pushed past him on the street, or who parked so close to his car in handicapped spots that his wheelchair wouldn't fit between them. But this was the first time I had witnessed someone who was just determined not to be inconvenienced by him or his disability.

A minute later, we were back at that end of the pool. "I'm sorry but we're going to need this ladder," I said again.

She turned and looked as Bob lingered on the bottom, in no hurry to come up. Then she closed her eyes, making a show of the effort it was taking to remain calm. Finally, just as Bob surfaced, she climbed up onto the deck, spraying water across his chair, and stomped off.

Bob took the regulator out of his mouth and leaned back to float. "Oh, that felt good. I might be able to do this."

"Great."

He looked up and nodded at the woman as she stormed into the locker room. "So what did you do to piss her off?"

"Nothing," I said. "I'm pretty sure it was you who pissed her off."

Bobby laughed. "Yeah, it probably was. You might not believe this but it isn't always easy being me."

He leaned back to float again. And that was the closest thing to a complaint I ever heard him make.

****

For dogs in New Hampshire, Pierce Island, at the mouth of the Piscataqua River in Portsmouth, is a mecca.

Dozens of them go crazy here, running free, barking, wrestling, chasing balls. Not surprisingly, the 50-yard stretch of grass between the parking lot and the water is a minefield of dog poop. I choose my steps accordingly.

"Hey, I finally made it here," someone called as I stepped out of my car.

I looked up and saw Andrea Dec, tall and thin, her drysuit already on, her brownish red hair pulled back in a loose ponytail.

"Andrea!" I said. "You've never dived here before?"

"Never, and I am so looking forward to it!"

I couldn't help but smile. Andrea is the kind of diver who comes out of the water, switches tanks and heads right back in. Sometimes she comes out after that and heads back in again. Conditions and temperatures don't seem to matter. She dives so much that anytime I see her away from the water, out of her drysuit, it takes me a second to recognize her – she just looks out of place.

Andrea and I also share a love of nudibranchs – one of the ocean's most incredible animals. And Pierce Island is one of the best places in the world to find them.

A dozen other divers were gearing up. I took a walk along their cars but didn't know any of them. We would all be heading in at the same time, though, because, as in Eastport, the tidal currents are strong and can only be dived at slack water.

To avoid the crush, I geared up slowly and let everyone head in first, including Andrea. Then I started across the field. Dogs barked and bounded about. A pair of yorkies charged past within inches of my legs, yipping and yapping. A black lab rushed up, dropped to the ground in an I-can't-wait-to-play-with-you posture, and began orbiting me in assorted sitting, standing and lying positions. Another dog – this one enormous – stood off to the side, watching with an expression that would have been incredibly intelligent if it weren't for the muddy tennis ball in its mouth.

I reached the water in one piece, just as the last of the other divers was disappearing down through a surge of bubbles. I took one last look at the canine chaos behind me, then headed under, too.

The water temperature has dropped and I can feel the cold pressing against my suit right through the thermals. The water is 34 degrees and visibility a dark 15 feet.

Even though the Piscataqua is a river, it's salt water – at least here at the mouth. Pieces of broken red brick cover the bottom in the shallows, then disappear under a blanket of kelp. The slope is gentle at first but at 20 feet it steepens and soon the kelp is replaced by thousands of tiny hydroids. They look like dandelions with thin stems and round, pink heads encircled by hair-like tentacles. They blanket the bottom, covering every rock and boulder. They're all I see in every direction.

The hydroids are like anemones. They use nematocysts to hunt, stinging microscopic plankton as it drifts by. All around me, plankton by the tens of thousands are being stung, ripped apart and eaten. Millions more are drifting by safely. Some are the larvae of bigger creatures – crabs, lobsters, sea stars, fish – but haven't morphed yet into whatever it is they'll eventually become. Others are what they are and always will be. And I can see none of them. They're all too small.

I settle down on a patch of gravel in front of a boulder the size of a washing machine. It's covered with hydroids. It takes a little while but finally I see a nudibranch in the tangle, up on the stalk of a hydroid, eating its head. Beautiful wine-red, finger-like projections known as cerata, rise up from the nudibranch's back and sway in the current. Each cerata is capped with an iridescent white tip. Across the world, the vast majority of nudibranchs are less than half an inch in length. This one is three inches.

The more I look, the more of them I see, until I see them everywhere. They're all big and heavy-bodied, cerata swaying as they move through and around and over hydroids, attacking and eating them. The hydroids' stinging nematocysts seem completely ineffective. But the nudibranchs aren't attacking in spite of the nematocysts – they're attacking for them.

Nudibranchs have no natural defenses. They're basically snails without shells. And a snail without a shell should be dinner for everything else down here. But nudibranchs are able to eat nematocysts without them firing, move them through their digestive tracts in their cerata all the way to the iridescent tips at the ends, where they're re-oriented to point outward and can be fired at anything that tries to attack them.

Think about this for a moment. For us to transplant an organ from one person to another takes teams of doctors and technicians, technology and drugs. And the transplant might not work. But nudibranchs are able to eat a body part from an entirely different animal and incorporate it into themselves.

I hover in close to one pair whose bodies are intertwined as if wrestling. They're actually mating. All nudibranchs are both male and female at the same time and any two of the same species can impregnate each other. The more I look, the more mating pairs I see, tangled together, some eating at the same time. If they could watch TV, too, they'd achieve George Costanza's trifecta. It won't be long before their white egg strings are woven in and around countless hydroid stems.

Within a few months, though, they will all be dead, their egg strings all that's left of them. The eggs will hatch and drift through the water for a while as plankton. Then it will be the hydroids feeding on them, stinging and ripping them apart, until the survivors settle on the bottom, morph into nudibranchs and the process begins again.

"That was unbelievable," Andrea said, while I poured a jug of warm water over my head. "I've never seen that many nudibranchs. I was yelling into my regulator!"

"I think I heard you," I said.

The tide had turned and all of the other divers were out of the water, too, laughing, shouting, comparing notes.

As I finished packing up, Andrea pulled me aside. "I found a ledge at Folly Cove yesterday that's covered with big salmon gilled nudibranchs."

Salmon gills were a species I often went years without seeing. "Where's the ledge?" I asked.

She spent the next few minutes trying to give directions but finally gave up. "I'll just take the day off and show you!" she said, her face lighting up.

****

I pulled into the dirt parking lot overlooking Folly Cove in Gloucester, Massachusetts – a small inlet squeezed between a rock cliff on its left side and a gentle slope of bedrock on its right. The beach at the head of the cove, below the parking lot, was an undependable one. Some years it was covered with sand and walking to and from the water was easy. Other years, storms pulled the sand away, leaving a field of slippery rocks that had to be crossed when the tide was out. For most of my dive life, the state of the tide and the beach made no difference. I dove when I wanted.

Then one morning I came and had the place to myself. The tide was midway between high and low. Long swells were rolling in, one after another, stirring up the bottom. I was wearing double tanks and as I walked over the rocks, hidden in shin-deep water, I got caught with one foot high on a slippery one, the other foot low on a slippery one, with a big swell rolling in. The wave hit and I went down like Joe Frazier after taking a right from George Foreman (in a Howard Cosell voice, think, "Down goes Frazier! Down goes Frazier! Down goes Frazier!").

The slippery rocks of Folly Cove at low tide. Carrying 100 pounds of dive gear and camera equipment across them is not fun.

My double tanks clanged off the rocks and I lay on my back turtle-like, clutching my fins in one hand, my camera in the other, as sand and seaweed from the next wave blasted over me. When it passed, I scrambled to my knees and tried to stand. But both feet were now slipping wildly on the rocks. I got hit full-force by the next wave and went down again with another clang. I tried to get up but slipped and went down again. And again – over and over.

As I lay there on my back spitting out sand and seaweed, I had one thing going for me: there was no one else in the cove to see – that is, unless someone had pulled in and parked after I walked down.

I didn't want to look but I had to know. In between waves, I craned my neck all the way back until I had a clear though upside-down view of the parking lot.

The good news was it was still empty. The bad news was that the driver's side door of my car was wide open.

That did it. In a fury, I pushed to my feet, turned around and managed to make my way over the slippery rocks back onto the beach.

Since then, I've only dived here at high tide, when the rocks are submerged enough that you can swim, rather than walk, over them.

I got out of my car and looked down at the water. It was lapping reassuringly high up on the beach. Two other cars were parked but Andrea was nowhere to be seen. Out on the right side of the cove, a red and white diver's flag bobbed up and down. That might have been her.

I checked my watch to see if I was late. As I did, Bobby Boyle pulled in, making his loop of the sites.

"Are you diving here?" he asked.

"Yeah. Do you know if either of these cars is Andrea's?"

Bob looked over and shook his head. "Give me a call when you're done and let me know how the viz is," he said as he backed out.

I geared up and walked down to the water. I was pretty sure I could find the ledge from Andrea's directions. The dive flag out on the right was now making a beeline straight in so I stood there waist-deep to see if it was her. Sure enough, when the flag reached the shallows, she and her buddy John popped up.

"I'm sorry," I said. "Was I late?"

"No," Andrea said, "this was just our first dive.

We're going to make a second one."

I looked out at the water, feeling the cold of it. It was going to take them at least 15 minutes to walk up to their cars, switch their tanks and walk back down. "I'll meet you out there," I said.

I inflated my BC and kicked backward on the surface all the way over to the left wall of the cove. The water was flat calm and I could see the clean, sandy bottom 30 feet down. I raised my BC hose, let out the air and dropped under.

I'm drifting down the vertical rock wall head-first, past a band of red seaweed, a colony of hydroids and shelves covered with urchins. At the sand, I settle on my knees. Visibility is 30 feet and the wall continues in both directions, left and right, beyond what I can see.

The bare rock is broken up here and there by swaths of a cream-colored tunicate. Unlike the tunicates in Eastport, this one is flat and attached to the rock, blanketing it in sheets. It looks like something someone vomited up after eating too much oatmeal. In places, it's tinged yellow. Up ahead, a large piece of it hangs loose from the rock, attached only along its upper edge while the rest fluffs slowly up and down in the water like a blanket.

It's *Didemnum vexillum*, an invasive species believed to have come here from Japan on the hulls and in the ballast water of ships. A few years ago, I had never seen it. Now it's everywhere. And it's covering more than just rock. It's overgrowing everything. A mass of blue mussels is surrounded, their dark shells flecked with it. A flat white sponge is completely enclosed, its edges being covered over. A frilled anemone is also encircled with no way to escape, while a sea peach has been engulfed, its shape still visible beneath, still sucking in and blowing out water through its siphons.

Invasive species are big news. They move into new environments and decimate native species. Lionfish are probably the best known of them, introduced to Florida and the Caribbean from the Pacific. They're now laying waste to everything around them (lionfish can eat up to 30 times their own stomach volume) and have gained worldwide press.

What happens, though, when an invasive isn't beautiful, or the environment it's moved into isn't a tourist destination? What happens when the invasive is a pukey mess that few people will ever see? I can tell you: almost nothing. *Didemnum vexillum* is crowding out local invertebrates throughout New England and has spread to Nova Scotia on the east coast and all the way up to Alaska on the west. It's also shown up in Ireland and the Mediterranean.

I move past a swath of it to a section of wall that juts out ten feet onto the sand at a right angle. I'm pretty sure this is Andrea's spot. There's no *Didemnum vexillum* here. There are hydroids, though, and I start searching through them for her salmon gilled nudibranchs.

I find nothing. I float up to the top of the rock. A brown sea raven is sitting here, holding something in its mouth. I move in closer but can't figure out what it has. The raven just watches.

Finally, I realize what it is – a massive tumor growing out of the sea raven's lower jaw. There's no way it can eat with that tumor in the way. Its metabolism is low enough now that it won't need to feed through the winter. But once the water warms – if it survives that long – it will need to hunt. At that point, it will either die of starvation or be eaten itself.

I hate to give up on the nudibranchs but I have less than half a tank of air left. I turn and start back along the wall at the sand. Then Andrea and John appear, swimming side by side. Andrea holds up a thumb and forefinger an inch apart, then points to her eyes. I'm terrible at deciphering hand signals but I think she's asking if I saw the nudibranchs.

I shake my head.

She takes my arm and leads me back out. Less than a minute later, we're at the same spot I just left, just feet from where I had looked. Sure enough, one of the rock faces – about 4 feet by six feet – is sprinkled with salmon gilled nudibranchs. There are at least ten of them – all an inch long and fat with white iridescent spots up and down their salmon-colored cerata. Some are eating. Some are curled up mating.

I can only stay a few minutes but I know where they are now and will be able to find them again.

I leaned against the side of my car in the parking lot with a cup of hot chocolate. My gear was stowed and I was dried off and dressed.

Andrea and John's flag was still well out on the left wall. Just then, John bubbled to the surface, probably low on air. Andrea stayed under, though. She's one of those divers who barely breathes and can make a tank last forever. While John swam above, the flag cut across the cove to the right side, then moved out along the rocks, then slowly started in.

Finally, they made it into the shallows. But even then, it took a few minutes for Andrea to surface. At last, she stood up in the water waist-deep and stared out at the cove for a long moment.

"I wish I had a third tank," she finally said, more to herself than to anyone else.

The next day I went back to photograph Andrea's nudibranchs. I spent the whole dive shooting them before drifting up to the top of that rock again. The sea raven with the tumor was still there. It hadn't moved an inch.

****

After an on-again, off-again start, the winter had taken a hard turn, with blisteringly cold air temperatures combining with one historic snowstorm after another. We were setting snow records left and right.

I hadn't been in the water in three weeks. On the first mild day, I drove to Folly, hoping the inevitable snowbank plowed between the parking lot and the beach wouldn't be too high to climb over.

It turned out there was no parking lot. The whole

thing was plowed in under ten feet of snow. I couldn't even see the water over it. There was no way I was going to dive but I wanted to at least get a look at the water. I climbed to the top of the snowbank and looked down. The entire cove, from one side to the other, from the beach out to the mouth, was jammed with pack ice.

I had never seen that before.

****

The policeman on the other side of the glass swiveled around in his chair. "What can I do for you?"

"I was hoping I could park at Canoe Beach," I said. "I don't live in Nahant."

There were only half a dozen parking spots at Canoe Beach and all were reserved for Nahant residents. They probably weren't expecting much in the way of beach traffic, though.

"What do you want to do there?" he asked.

"Make a dive," I said. "A scuba dive."

He looked at me skeptically over his glasses and for a few moments said nothing. He folded his hands together. "How long will you be?"

"About an hour."

He thought about it, then nodded. "Okay," he said, swiveling back to his work, "have a nice dive."

The parking lot was plowed out and the cove at Canoe Beach was ice-free but the water had that gray, steely look it sometimes gets in the winter. It was not inviting. For a second, I thought about getting back in my car and driving home.

But just then, the sun broke through the clouds and the water looked a little softer, a little bluer. And I couldn't help but wonder what was happening under there right at that moment. I geared up, climbed over a snowbank and headed in.

I've just dipped under and my fingers are already stinging with cold. So are my lips. At the same time, shafts of brilliant sunlight are angling down onto a pink rubble bottom that stretches out in front of me, crisp and clear. I can see the dark, craggy ledge that marks the right side of the cove 40 feet away. Straight out, even farther off, a rock spire rises up from the bottom like a chimney. Beyond it, the outlines of two more rise up, as well. It's like a small forest.

I swim straight out to them. The first is 25 feet high, about 30 feet around, and is covered with tufts of short brown seaweed. Here and there, patches of tiny white anemones, each the size of a pencil eraser, are scattered over it. The spires behind it are much the same.

I move up off the bottom and come face-to-face with a yellow sea raven lying on a rocky shelf. Most sea ravens, like the two in Eastport or the one at Folly, are brownish red for camouflage. But this one stands out like a neon light. Any predator can see it. It's just a different approach to camouflage, though. The yellow falsely advertises it as unappetizing, perhaps even poisonous.

The raven is completely torpid in the cold. I could pick it up in my hands and it wouldn't move. That's not surprising – I can feel the bitter temperature moving right through my thermals and into me. It's hard to believe anything can survive in this cold without layer upon layer of blubber. But the sea raven can because it has chemicals similar to antifreeze actually pumping through its blood, keeping it from freezing solid.

I leave the raven and circumnavigate the base of the spire until I reach a dark opening large enough to squeeze through. Camera first, I kick into a small cave inside shaped like a teepee. It's dark but not pitch black. I switch on my lights and sweep them along the walls. They're covered with frilled anemones, almost all of them orange.

There's one long crevice running horizontally through the wall a few feet above the sand. I twist my lights into it. The crevice is about two feet deep and something is moving inside. I push my lights farther in. It's filled with cunner – a beautiful brown and gold fish. There are about 30 of them, all well over a foot in length, pressed back against the rock, moving slowly away from me en masse. Cunner are common around here during the summer but I've never seen them during the winter. This must be why: they find a protected place to hide.

The cunner aren't torpid but they're very close and I don't want to bother them anymore than I already have. I back out through the entrance into open water again.

I'm now so cold that I'm wondering if my drysuit is leaking. But my thermals don't feel wet. I check my computer for the first time – the water is 29 degrees! (Salt water doesn't freeze until 28.) I've only been in for 20 minutes but this is enough. I check my compass, set a course back to the beach and start kicking in.

****

Every year, dive shows and conventions are put on across the country – Chicago, Long Beach, Dallas, Orlando, Las Vegas. Most are held in the winter and early spring when the majority of divers aren't diving and need some alternative fix. They're weekends of hands-on seminars, daytime presentations and evening film fests. Topics can cover anything ocean-related, from whale and shark conservation, to underwater police investigations, to vintage gear, to the planning of far-off dive trips.

The first time I was invited to speak at one was the Boston Sea Rovers show, one of the oldest and best in the country. I had just published my first book, *A Shore Diving Guide to New England*, and the show was to be its debut.

Looking back, I was pretty nervous beforehand. The prospect of speaking in front of a convention room full of people I didn't know was not a pleasant one. But I started off with a small joke and the audience broke up. All of a sudden I realized that I did know them – they were divers, they loved being underwater as much as I did and all they wanted was to get pumped for the upcoming season. I've spoken there, and at other shows,

The mountains of snow at Pierce Island, dwarfing passersby.
The water is just to the left, out of the picture.

every year since.

I would be speaking there again tomorrow, and Ed and Joe had come in a day early to squeeze in a dive at Pierce Island.

"Holy crap!" Ed said, staring up at the mountain of snow in the parking lot. It was a good 40 feet high and stretched 150 feet in either direction. It even had a road on it for trucks to take to the top to drop off more.

"Joe," Ed yelled, "you have to see this!"

Joe came around the line of parked cars, his dry-suit half on, and looked up at it. "Holy crap!" He pulled on his suit the rest of the way and then he and Ed started scrambling up it. We were going to do some climbing before getting in the water.

I'm gliding down a few feet over the broken bricks and the tangle of kelp and then out over the massive field of pink hydroids. Visibility is 15 feet and big, fat nudibranchs are everywhere, their red cerata swaying in the current. Ed is ten feet away and I can hear him yelling into his regulator. I don't think he's ever seen nudibranchs this big or in such numbers. Joe is farther down and his fins disappear into the gloom.

At 50 feet, I cut across the slope and swim parallel to the shore. After a couple of minutes, the hydroids thin out and the gravel bottom is replaced by a sheer rock wall dropping straight down, covered with frilled anemones. Hundreds of them are packed together – some brown, some orange, some white. They're grouped by color, rarely intermingling. This is cloning in action. Frilled anemones can split off pieces of themselves that grow into genetically identical anemones.

I drop down the wall and settle on a small ledge. A few feet up, two groups of anemones – one brown, the other white – have come together, separated by fractions of an inch. Neither can expand any more with the other there. One of the brown anemones at the intersection, and two of the whites, have extended long tentacles out from inside their shorter ones and are dragging them across anemones on the other side. This is a battle line. All of the anemones on it – and only the anemones on it – have these long, nematocyst-filled tentacles designed specifically for fighting, to try to force the other side back and make more room for themselves. But they'll only use them against anemones of the same sex. If they find themselves pressed up against an anemone of the opposite sex, they'll put their differences aside. They can reproduce sexually as well as asexually, and who knows, they may get lucky.

I rise up from the ledge and move diagonally across the wall when something flashes out in front of me and hits me in the chest.

Startled, I scull backward just as a big lumpfish swishes back into the rocks and turns to face me. Lumpfish are aptly named for the lumps and bumps that cover their bodies. But the name doesn't begin to capture their strangeness. This one is 15 inches long and just as high, with bright blue skin. It has no dorsal fin – just a series of even bigger bumps along its top ridge.

Suddenly, it blasts out of the rocks again and slams headfirst into my camera housing – behind which I have about $5,000 worth of equipment. And just like that, this lumpfish and I have a problem.

It must be guarding a nest of eggs in the rocks and I'm too close. Male lumpfish protect their eggs – constantly fanning them to keep them aerated and forcing potential predators away – until just before they hatch. The lumpfish blasts out again, aiming straight at my housing, and I turn and slap it aside. It zips back into the rocks.

I swing out and away from the wall, trying to put some ground between us, and back over the field of hydroids. I settle down on a bare spot of gravel and check to make sure my housing's not leaking. As I do, I see a mass of round green eggs tucked into the hydroid stems in front of me. Sculpin eggs. They must be very close to hatching and the sculpin guarding them must have already moved on – otherwise I'd be slam-dancing with him right now, too. I lean in for a closer look. And as I do, a tiny pair of sculpin eyes stares out at me from inside of each.

Later that night, my wife Daisy and I went to a reception party for the show's speakers. Bobby was sitting in a corner surrounded by people. He didn't usually come to these. They were too late at night and there were too many stairs to be negotiated. I pulled up a chair beside him.

"Bonaire's coming up," he said, when the crowd around him started to thin. "I can't wait to get down there. I need some time away from the snow."

I nodded, a little jealous I wouldn't be going with him. Unfortunately, he and I hadn't been able to get back in the pool since the day in January, so he wasn't even going to try to get in the water. "What's your talk on tomorrow?" he asked.

"Diving in Canada."

"Ah, great, cold water stuff. Can't wait." He leaned in closer. "Can you give me a hand getting out of here? I'm tired and no one seems to know how to work the wheelchair lift."

"Sure," I said. I started maneuvering his chair through the room but it took us another half-hour to work our way past all of the people who wanted to talk to him. Finally we made it to the wheelchair lift in a back stairway.

The control looked simple enough. But it wasn't. I spent the next five minutes pushing the button and trying to get the lift to move while Bob sank deeper into his wheelchair. At last, I had to go off to find someone on staff who could work it. But Bob was right – no one knew how to make it move. At that point, the stairwell was crowded with cooks, waiters and coat check people and the air felt hot and close.

"We'll pick up you up and carry you down," one of them said.

"No, don't do that," Bobby said. "I don't want to be picked up."

"It will be easy," someone else said, "we'll just put two guys on each side."

Through a forest of arms, I could see Bob getting jostled. "He doesn't want to be picked up," I said.

They went back to fumbling with the control.

Finally, the one woman in Massachusetts who seemed to know how to work the lift showed up and it instantly sprang to life. The stairwell exploded with cheers. Bobby was too tired to smile.

"Are you sure you're okay?" I asked when he was in his car. "I could drive you, with Daisy following in our car."

"I'm fine," he smiled. "I'm just tired. I'll see you tomorrow."

The next morning, I walked into the room at Sea Rovers where I would be speaking. As always at dive shows, the energy was great. Ed and Edna were sitting up front. I picked out Joe's big smile somewhere in the middle of the room, sitting beside his wife Connie. Bobby was parked in his chair at the back wall. Andy Martinez, who had just spoken before me and was one of Bobby's closest friends, stood beside him.

"All right," I said, as the lights dimmed and an image of Jack Nicholson, frozen solid at the end of *The Shining* appeared on-screen. "Let's talk about diving in Canada, eh!"

Spring

The inlet at Manasquan, New Jersey cuts into the shoreline between two long jetties that stretch out into the ocean. It was early April and the morning air felt soft and warm. A young woman practiced yoga by herself on a mat on the beach, while rows of fishermen stood back-to-back on the jetty closest to me, half of them casting into the inlet, the other half casting into the ocean. A low fog was rolling in over the water.

The jetties here start off as your standard line of boulders. About three-quarters of the way out, though, the boulders give way to a jumble of massive concrete shapes called dolosse that look like knuckle bones from a giant game of jacks. Rather than blocking waves, they dissipate their force by allowing only part of them through.

After checking the sea conditions, I walked back to my car and geared up, then made my way around the handrail separating the sidewalk from the water, down the rocks and into the inlet.

A group of locals gathered at the railing behind me.

The Manasquan Jetty, looking in toward the beach from the end. The inlet side of the jetty is off to the left, and the ocean side is off to the right. In the foreground are dolosse, covered with graffiti.

"Don't freeze to death," a woman called, getting a few laughs from the crowd.

A boy leaned over the rail. "Don't get eaten." Even more laughter.

"Don't scare off the fish," said a big guy standing between two fishing poles. That one really busted them up.

I'm in a wetsuit for the first time this year and cool water is seeping in. Other than the first trickle down my back, it feels great.

Visibility is 30 feet and the jetty's boulders

slope down in front of me. They're almost bare except for seaweed and barnacles. Small hermit crabs are scurrying along the bottom. A big toadfish – thick-lipped, heavy-bodied and looking like it was squished down and flattened a bit – turns and swims into one of the crevices between the boulders. A crab, its shell speckled rose and yellow, springs up into the water column and uses its rear legs like paddles to swim off.

I poke my head into a crevice and shine my lights in. Nothing but barnacles. Then something hits me hard on the butt. I push out and turn around. A striped bass – two feet long, silver, and lined with seven or eight dark bars on each side – is staring at me. A second one the same size hovers just behind it, motionless except for the sculling of its pectoral fins. And the fisherman at the railing was worried I'd scare them off.

It's these fish that he and the other guys casting from the jetty want. Stripers are big, fast and taste good. Or at least that's what I'm told. In one of life's ironies, I'm allergic to fish and have no idea what a striper tastes like. I reach out to this one but it veers off and swims deeper into the channel. The second one follows. I don't know why it hit me on the butt.

A moment later, the two reappear, moving in tandem, coming in close. I reach out again and they glide around me, keeping their distance. I turn back to the boulders and they instantly swim up alongside and stare into the rocks. They know divers pull lobsters from crevices and kick up crabs with their fins. They're hoping for an easy meal.

I pull myself hand-over-hand along the bottom row of boulders heading seaward. The stripers swim off.

A lone one swishes in close then zips off, too. Up ahead, another pair, smaller than the first, hangs in the water a few feet above the sand. A loose school of about 12 swims by farther out in the channel.

I move away from the boulders. A large lion's mane jelly pulses by just a few feet beneath the surface. Its bell is a foot in diameter, with a thick swath of brownish-orange tentacles reaching down a foot or so, and dozens of longer, string-like tentacles extending down several feet more. It's so close to the surface that it's being buffeted by the waves. First it's spun, then it's flipped. Then it rights itself. Its long tentacles should be tangled in knots but the water flow between them is enough to keep them apart. And any that do get tangled will just break off and re-grow.

A tautog (they call them blackfish here) – beefy and dark – sees me and immediately swims off. As it does, it keeps turning back to see if I'm following. It's hard to respect a fish like this.

I move back in toward the boulders and continue along them offshore until they're replaced by dolosse and the jetty turns into a dark maze of concrete legs. I shine my lights in but if there's any life in there, I don't see it.

At the far end of the jetty, sunlight streams down on the sand. Three sea robins – primitive looking fish with dinosaur-like plates armoring their heads – are settled down in front of me. All are a foot in length and colored to blend in with the sand. Two rise up and start to 'walk' away in different directions on what look like bony fingers at the front edge of their pectoral fins.

I swim in close to one and it fans out its wing-like pectorals fully – brown and blue and yellow – lifts off the bottom and glides away. I turn back to the one that didn't move. It looks at me, then wriggles straight down into the sand until only the top of its head and its brilliant blue eyes are visible.

I head back in toward the beach on the ocean side of the jetty. There was no surge inside the inlet but now I'm swinging back and forth three feet with each swell that passes overhead and then washes back out. Sand and seaweed and glittering schools of small silver fish are swinging back and forth with me. Sometimes I swing forward while the layer of sand under me is swinging backward. If I were prone to sea sickness, I'd be vomiting into my regulator right now.

Each of the swells hits the dolosse full force, dashing against them and washing down in a rain of bubbles. Each time, four or five stripers rush in and stop just outside the wash. Any crabs caught up in it will be swept off the bottom and be easy pickings.

The dolosse soon turn to boulders again. Something *plops* above me. I keep moving in along the rocks, not really thinking about it, until I hear it *plop* just above me again. A fisherman on the jetty must be casting at my flag for reasons unknown. If he hooks it, we'll be tied together and I'll have to surface to cut his line.

I see more than hear another *plop* farther ahead, followed by a slipstream of tiny bubbles. It's a fishing lure jigging back to the surface. A striper dashes up to it but turns and swims off. A minute later the same thing happens. And then again.

Finally, I reach the shallows and set down on the sand in about eight feet of water. The surge here is minimal. I've circumnavigated the jetty but still don't want to come out. The water feels so soft and the sun is so bright.

Three young boys are standing on top of the jetty, rippling with the surface of the water. All three are pointing at me and gesturing back to someone on the beach. I wave up to them. For a second, they freeze – then start jumping and waving too.

I came out on the beach only a short distance from where I had gone in. I walked to my car and found the group at the railing still there.

"Well," the big guy between the two poles said, "you scared 'em away."

"No, I didn't," I said. "They're down there." And just like that, I had everyone's attention.

"You saw them?"

"I did. I even saw them checking out your lures and swimming off."

I pulled a jug of fresh water from my trunk, unscrewed it and poured it over my head.

No one said anything for a while but it was like I could hear the wheels turning in their heads.

"What else did you see?" someone finally asked.

****

"Let me guess, you're here to see Bob," the nurse said. "He gets more visitors than anyone I've ever seen." She pointed down the hallway. "Last door on the right."

Bobby was sleeping when I walked in, hooked up

to some kind of monitor and breathing through a tube. His trip to Bonaire had not gone well. He had developed a lung infection, had to be medivacked to a Miami hospital, then waited there for weeks until he could be booked on a special flight back to Boston and to this rehab center not far from his home.

He woke up a few minutes after I walked in. He couldn't talk with the tube in his throat but he launched into a silent monologue of sign language and lip moving, none of which I could decipher. He tried writing instead but that left him drained and frustrated, so we switched back to 'talking.'

For minutes at a stretch, he mouthed words, gestured with his hands and used facial expressions to emphasize points. He'd stop to rest, then launch into another story.

At some point, I started wondering if he was playing a joke on me and none of it meant anything. I couldn't put it past him. But then his nurse walked in. He mouthed silently to her and gestured with his hands and she repeated back what she thought he had said – his pillows were too high, he was having trouble sleeping at night and he wanted his physical therapists to come in. He nodded. It was like watching a magician pull rabbits out of a hat.

When she left, I moved back beside him, determined to do better. "Bobby, did you tell me that Jacques Cousteau made a dive near your shop once?"

Bobby's face lit up. He launched into another monologue and I focused on him with every fiber of my being. I was concentrating so hard I probably could have mentally bent a spoon. But I couldn't understand what he was saying. By the end of the story, the only thing I knew for sure was that, yes, Jacques Cousteau had once made a dive near his shop. Maybe.

His physical therapists then walked in and began communicating with him effortlessly.

****

I stood on the boat ramp at White Horse Beach in Plymouth, Massachusetts, a few miles north of Cape Cod. A hundred yards offshore, a massive rock rose up from the water with a U.S. flag painted on it.

When I was 11, I had spent a week at this beach with family friends. They had an older boy who had another friend with him. They were the big kids and they were into spearfishing. They had masks and fins and snorkels that were rubber and black and rugged. And I yearned for them.

I still had the white plastic mask I had bought at Lake Mamanasco. I still made tub dives with it. I still brought it with me to free swims at the Boy's Club. But I didn't have it with me that week and that was probably for the best. As much as I loved it, it wouldn't have measured up. To be a real diver, I needed a rubber mask. A black one.

Every day that week, the two older boys snorkeled out on the surface to Flag Rock, spears in hand, jackknifing down in search of prey. I was awestruck. It didn't matter that neither of them ever speared anything.

On my last day there, they managed to scrounge

up an extra mask for me. I swam out on the surface with them, not quite able to keep up since I didn't have fins. But I couldn't have been happier. It was my first time snorkeling in the ocean – my first time seeing for myself what was down there. I saw that Flag Rock was like an iceberg, even bigger below the surface than it was above. I saw boulders scattered across the yellow sand. I saw the seaweed that rose up from them, thick and impenetrable all the way to the surface.

I was scared shitless.

There was no way to know what was lurking inside that seaweed. And with no concrete information to go on, my 11-year-old imagination ran wild.

Minutes after swimming out, I had to turn around and swim back. I even had to take off the mask to avoid looking at the seaweed. It was humiliating. For as long as I could remember, I had wanted to be a diver. When I finally got the chance, I chickened out.

The next day, my mother showed up to take me home. With some distance between the seaweed and me, my fear of it faded and I decided my time underwater counted. I was a diver.

I stood on the ramp that morning, older and a little wiser. I had no tank with me. I didn't want one. I just had my mask, fins, and snorkel. I wanted to see the place again from the surface, just as I had when I was 11.

I put on my wetsuit and snorkeled out, expecting it all to look so much smaller than I remembered. But it didn't. The boulders and the yellow sand between them looked exactly the same. Flag Rock was the same, too – massive on the surface and even bigger underwater. The only thing missing was the seaweed. It was too early in the year for it.

I took a few deep breaths and jackknifed down, settling on the bottom at the base of Flag Rock. I had waited a very long time to be in this spot and I stayed until I couldn't hold my breath any longer.

****

"Woo-hoo!" Ed said, coming out of his house as I pulled in. Edna was right behind him, followed by their black Newfies, Levi and Halo.

A few minutes later, I dropped my duffel bag in their living room.

"You'll be sleeping here," Ed said, pointing at a couch. "Levi and Halo usually sleep here so you might have to fight them for it."

I looked at the two massive dogs staring at me almost eye-to-eye, drooling, with big doggy smiles on their faces, and realized that the couch was far from a sure thing.

"You want to dive from the boat or from the beach?" Ed asked. "Never mind, let's do both."

With a full load of passengers, marine life shuttling in and out of the touch tank, and Ed at full volume, the 54-foot *Starfish Enterprise* is something to behold. When it's just three of you, though, with all of the seating stowed, it's impressive in a whole different way: the back deck stretches out behind you like a football field, while the beam feels like two boats have been lashed together side-by-side.

We motored out through Bar Harbor to Egg Rock (off the New England coast, there's an 'Egg Rock' every few miles). When we finished gearing up, Ed grabbed a white line off the deck. "I'm going to bring this with us just in case there's a current," he said. "You want to hold onto the other end and pull us up when we're done?" he asked Edna.

Edna nodded.

Ed began coiling the line and singing softly to himself.

> *I'll be swinging on a line with Jerry Shine,*
> *just swinging on a line with Jerry Shine,*
> *I'll be swinging on a line with Jerry Shine,*
> *at the bottom of the sea.*

The song then looped around and repeated until we stepped off the back deck and into the water.

We're descending feet-first through dark, greenish water and the bottom comes into view just before we touch it, 60 feet down. Ed's line is paying out behind him at a 45-degree angle back to the boat.

There's nothing here on the bottom but rock. Not rocks, as in plural. Rock – as in one smooth, undulating ledge for as far as I can see, which is about 20 feet in all directions. There's absolutely nothing on it. It looks like a mountaintop that's been scoured by the wind and weather. Despite the apparent lifelessness (there is life – I just don't see it), the bottom is mind-blowing, like a lunar landscape rolling this way and that, with cracks and crevices and dips and gullies.

I don't want to get separated from Ed and the line, and end up surfacing a mile from the boat, so I'm staying close. I follow him over the rock to a massive crack, about six feet wide and ten feet deep. I drop in and stare down its length. It runs through the ledge and disappears into the gloom. Ed drops in in front of me and starts kicking forward.

Unlike the top of the ledge, the crack offers some protection from the elements and its sides are dotted with colonies of hydroids and sea vases – sea peach-like tunicates that are elongated and white. Sea stars – at least ten of them – are glommed together on top of one of another, feeding on something underneath.

I take a few shots of the sea stars, then look up. Ed is gone. I look down the crack. Nothing. I rise up over the lip onto the ledge and look left and right. Still nothing. This is the problem with being an underwater photographer: while your face is in your camera, your buddies invariably swim off. Ed and I dive alone all the time but when you've decided to stick together, you have to stick together. Otherwise you won't know if your buddy is in trouble or just swam off. Plus, Ed has the line.

I know he wouldn't have left the crack without checking that I was behind him first, so I keep moving forward through it. A minute later, Ed re-appears, coming back for me.

The rest of the dive goes much like this. We stay

in the crack, which cuts through the ledge for as far as we swim and more, and there's a moderate amount of life in it: a northern red anemone here, a few crabs and a couple of nudibranchs there. It doesn't sound exciting but the ledge itself is worth the price of admission. I love topography that's the same above the water and below – identical landscapes in opposite environments.

An hour into the dive, Ed signals that it's time to head up. I grab the bit of line dangling behind him and he gives a few pulls to Edna. Then the slack pulls taut and we're being hauled up, just over the ledge first, then straight up through the water like an amusement park ride.

Ed took his time motoring the *Starfish Enterprise* back to the dock, making passes in close to Mount Desert Island and Acadia National Park. Sheer rock cliffs towered above us. Long pebble beaches stretched out between them. Pine forests ran right up to the water. In places, familiar looking expanses of bare, undulating ledge broke through.

By the time we made it back to Ed and Edna's, we had to hustle right out again. Ed had scheduled an underwater hockey game at a local pool and seemed very excited that I was going to play. The truth was that I had never played underwater hockey. I didn't even know the rules. But I had been a decent hockey player when I was a kid. And I was pretty good underwater. So I figured I was going to dominate.

It turns out that underwater hockey is played across the shallow end of a pool. Cones are set up at each end to mark the nets and each player has a little stick to move a puck along the bottom. You can stand up anytime you want but you have to be underwater to touch the puck.

Ed chose up the sides. There were eight of us but for some reason the teams were him, another guy and me against the remaining five.

Now to be honest, I was in terrible shape. I wasn't far removed from having broken two vertebrae in a surfing accident and I hadn't run or lifted in over a year.

As I stood there in the pool waiting for the game to start, I looked around at the other players. Except for Ed and me, they were all in their twenties. And they had that eye of the tiger. The guy across from me looked like he spent most of his waking hours in the gym and ate nothing but spinach. He was hyperventilating and shaking his arms out like a competitive swimmer before a race. The guy beside him looked like his big brother and stared off into space with his eyes opened scarily wide.

"All right," Ed said. "Everybody ready?" He tossed the puck into the middle of the pool. "GO!"

I dived under and torpedoed straight at it. I got to the puck first and corralled it with my stick when someone grabbed my arm and pulled it back. Someone else ripped my stick away and elbowed me in the ribs. A third guy dove straight over me, kicking me in the head on the way by. Holy crap! I stood up, woozy and dizzy, and looked back. The other team was already celebrating a goal and Ed was staring at me with a confused look. He had thought he was getting a ringer.

I looked up at the clock. We had the pool for another 58 minutes.

An hour later, I climbed out of the pool a different person than I had gone in. At some point, the old competitive juices had bubbled up and I made a couple of end-to-end, Bobby Orr-like underwater drives. But I felt like a zombie. And not a zombie in a fast-zombie movie; a zombie in one where they walk around slack-jawed, with one leg dragging.

It was now ten o'clock but Ed wanted to stop for Thai food. As we drove through Bar Harbor in the Diver Ed Mobile – the one decked out with oversized stickers of underwater superheroes – people on the sidewalks called and waved, other drivers beeped. It had been this way all day. Ed's like the mayor here, forever participating in parades and clean-ups, inviting kids' groups and elementary schools onto his boat. I'm not even sure he realizes how popular he is. But if he doesn't, he should.

Fifteen years ago, a winter storm raged through Bar Harbor, driving all but one of the moored boats up onto the rocks. Ed's boat at the time, the *Seal*, was a complete loss. His insurance company had no plans to give him enough to replace it and the bank had no plans to loan him enough to rebuild it. Ed thought the Dive-In Theater was dead.

Then word got around town that he and Edna needed help. Like a scene out of *It's A Wonderful Life*, people began stepping up. A local improvement society held a benefit dinner for them. So did a dive club. Then the College of the Atlantic did, too. People began donating valuables to auction off. A friend put on a variety show. Hundreds of dollars turned into thousands of dollars, which turned into tens of thousands of dollars.

"At that point, we had no choice," Ed laughs. "We had to figure out a way to make it work." They drew up plans to have a new boat built just the way they wanted – plans that turned into the *Starfish Enterprise*.

Inside the Thai restaurant, Ed was rolling along, talking about the boat, the Dive-In Theater, the town, and life in general, while Edna giggled at his jokes. I was having a hard time keeping my head up.

At last we made it back to their place and Edna made up a bed on the couch. Levi and Halo looked on excitedly. Then I got in.

The two massive newfies sat and stared at me from the floor, their faces inches away. Halo gave up first, walking off to some other part of the house, not to be seen again. Levi, however, stayed, not sure what to make of this. He sat in the near-dark, breathing loudly. I could see the silhouette of his head, the size of a basketball, and the big gloopy string of drool hanging from his mouth. His tail thumped away on the floor.

As much as he missed his bed, he seemed to want me to enjoy it. I looked into Levi's shiny black eyes, big-hearted and friendly, and thought how much better the world would be if more of us were like him. Ed and Edna were like Levi – without the drool. Well, Edna didn't drool. I had seen Ed come out of the water with his face covered in it.

Just then, Levi leaned in and gave me the sloppiest kiss I could ever have imagined, then padded off into the darkness.

He wasn't done, though. Throughout the night, he came back regularly to make sure there still wasn't room for him. Each time he saw that there wasn't, he planted another big, drooly kiss on my face before walking off. I started waking up just enough to pull up the blanket when I heard him coming. His tongue would then swipe along it, searching for me. I'd drift back to sleep and the blanket would slip back down – until his next visit.

At some point the next morning, I heard Ed in the kitchen. "What do you think we should do?" he asked softly. It was the first time I had ever heard him whisper.

I forced my eyes open. Sunlight was pouring in through the windows. "I'm awake," I yelled, and rolled off the couch to get dressed. When I was done, I looked up and saw Levi and Halo on the couch, smiling and wagging their tails.

I let Ed and Edna go off to eat by themselves. Breakfast is a big deal for them. On trips we've taken together, they come back from whatever restaurant they breakfasted at with tales of whatever spread had been laid out before them. Ed's voice soars while he describes chocolates and pastries and muffins they had their pick of, while Edna talks just under him, adding detail.

I, on the other hand, couldn't care less about breakfast. At best, I'll puree a banana and some peanut butter into a smoothie. It wasn't right to inflict that on them.

When Ed and Edna returned, sated, excited, and with stories of the stacks of pancakes they had ordered, we headed off for a shore dive.

A few minutes after leaving their house, we pulled into Bartlett's Landing on Mount Desert Island. Dark skies were threatening and a blanket of fog covered the water. A long gangway led down to a small fleet of fishing boats, tied up to a series of slips. Green lobster traps were stacked everywhere, waiting for the water to warm and the lobsters to come back.

"This isn't really much of a dive," Ed said. "But you'll love it."

We geared up at the cars, made our way down the steep gangway and strode in between the stacks of traps.

I'm sinking through darkish water and hit the bottom just 15 feet down. Muck billows up around me. The current is running just a bit, though, and in a moment, pulls the muck away.

Cerianthids – white, flower-like animals that look like anemones – are everywhere on the bottom. They live in tubes buried in the muck and extend their tentacles up to feed. When need be, they can retract at lightning speed back into the tubes. They do it so fast that you don't see it. One second they're there. The next second, they're not.

Toad crabs, looking like giant spiders, are also everywhere, dozens of them, moving in and around the cerianthids. I've already lost track of Ed. I see no rock or ledge anywhere but, as always around boatyards, the bottom is littered with trash: five-gallon buckets, pots and pans, engine parts. All of it is covered with life – tiny outcroppings of color on the brown muck.

Each piece of trash starts with a base layer of pink coralline algae. A five-gallon bucket in front of me looks like it was originally blue, and the contrast between it and the pink is striking, even artistic. An orange sheathing tunicate has spread across the bottom of the bucket and is working its way around the edge and up the sides. There are barnacles on it, too, their tiny filament arms pulsing out rhythmically to catch plankton. A single small sea peach is attached to the bucket and a purplish blood star is out about to crawl up over it. A larger common star is spread out along the top rim.

I move away and pass over a weird sponge I've never seen before. It's the size of a cantaloupe but irregularly shaped and with the consistency of styrofoam. It looks yellow but its surface seems to have turned a grayish-green. Ed later identifies it as a fig sponge.

Three whelks – large snails with pointed, conical shells – are attaching cream-colored egg capsules that look like tiny purses to the side of an old vice. The whelks are only a few inches in length and the egg mass is five or six times their size. Watching the eggs come out of them is like watching a dozen clowns come out of a Mini Cooper. Each female will lay up to 2,000 of these purses, which expand once they're out in the water. Each of the purses holds up to 3,000 eggs. Almost none will produce a whelk that reaches adulthood, though, or the ocean would be overrun by them.

I have no idea where I am but the current is

building so I float to the surface to take a look. The docks are only 50 feet away. Edna is crouched on the shoreline in the fog, photographing something. Ed's bubbles are roiling the surface just ahead of me, moving toward the ramp we'll be using as an exit. I head back down and sit on the bottom. A blanket of silt rises up and envelopes me. But I'm in no hurry to leave.

****

Lines of swells were rolling in, building in the shallows and then curling and breaking with a crash. I stood on the cobble at the water's edge of Gloucester's eastern shore, fins in hand, waiting for a break in the waves.

After a few false starts, I saw an opening and rushed in. In waist-deep water, still in the surf zone, I pulled on my fins as fast as I could as the next wave barreled in, then dove under as it swept overhead. Its pull dragged me back toward the beach but I kicked as hard as I could and made it out of the shallows and past the surf.

In seconds, I'm into calm water, over rivers of sand, sun-dappled and broken up by solitary boulders. The slope of the bottom away from the shore is almost imperceptible. Small cunner, three or four inches in length, are flitting about the boulders everywhere. Just ahead, a brown sea raven sits on the bottom. It doesn't move when it sees me, or even when I get close, and I press down on the sand in front of it. Its mouth is strangely open. I peer inside. There's a live crab deep in its throat! The crab sees me from behind the sea raven's teeth and raises its claws to defend itself.

The sea raven opens its mouth even wider, sucks in water and regurgitates, trying to spit the crab out. But the crab spreads its claws wide and holds itself in.

As tough as the inside of the fish's mouth must be, having a live crab in there can't be good. I try to grab the raven by its tail to hold it upside-down and shake the crab out but the raven scoots away. It rises up off the bottom, turns itself upside-down and regurgitates again. The crab comes spitting out and lands on the sand as the raven swishes back down, as well. The two lie on the bottom within inches of each other, face-to-face and dazed.

It takes a minute but the raven gets a hold of itself first and swims off, no longer hungry. The crab looks shocked and still doesn't move. Finally, it scurries away sideways.

A school of pollock is swirling overhead, just below the surface. Moon snails, cunner, striped bass, rock crabs, green crabs, and hermit crabs are everywhere. The sand is bathed in sunlight. Spring has definitely sprung.

Something big is swimming a few feet off the bottom about 50 feet away, just beyond my visibility. I follow behind it, trying not to look interested, trying not to spook it. A minute later, though, I'm no closer.

I pause at a boulder and pretend to look in a different direction. I move to the next boulder and do the same. And the next. Little by little, it's paying off. I'm within about 40 feet of it but still can't tell what it is. It's about six feet long and impossibly thin but its size and shape seem to change.

Finally, I see that it's not one fish but two, swimming together, one just ahead of the other. They're sturgeon – skittish fish that I've only seen twice before, both times briefly. They look like something from the Jurassic Period, with long, paddle-like noses and bony scutes covering their bodies. They're best known for their eggs, used to make caviar.

These two seem a little less wary than the others I've seen but only marginally so. After swimming behind them for five minutes, slowing down when they look my way, speeding up when they look away, I'm within 25 feet. The architecture of their armor is incredible, with high, hard ridges lining their tops and running down their sides.

As I follow, the pair changes direction, heads back toward the shore, then cuts a long gentle arc around until they're moving perpendicular to me, with our paths set to cross. I put my head down, trying not to frighten them, and pass over a patch of sand in a circle of rocks. A huge sculpin sits in the middle of it, holding another sculpin, only slightly smaller, in its mouth, perpendicular to itself. Its teeth are clamped over the smaller one's head and much of its face. As I pass overhead, the smaller one looks up at me with its one exposed eye.

I'm now torn. The sculpin are locked in a life-and-death struggle and it's impossible not to feel for the smaller one. But I want to get close to the sturgeon and swim with them.

I put my head down and keep swimming. The

sturgeon have scooted ahead, though, not wanting to cross paths and I'm more than 30 feet back again.

I take up a zig-zag course behind them. They're now more aware of me and pick up the pace. They cut to the right again and head offshore. I cut with them but they cut to the left, then to the right and in an instant they're gone.

I stop on the bottom and stare into the empty water where they were, hoping they'll re-appear. They don't. They're gone. I turn and look back at the boulders, trying to remember where the sculpin are. But the boulders all look the same. There's no way I'm going to find them again. I've missed out on them, too.

A few minutes later, I start back in toward the beach, frustrated and bracing myself for a white-water exit.

I sat at the back of my car on the edge of the trunk, still aggravated. A woman approached on the sidewalk, walking fast and talking loudly on her cell, dictating orders á la Meryl Streep in *The Devil Wears Prada*. She saw my tank and then me dripping wet and did a double-take. She lowered the phone.

"Did you just come out of the water?" she demanded.

"I did."

Without looking away, she raised the phone back to her face. "I'll call you back."

She stared at me for a long moment, one finger tapping the top of the cell. "So what did you see down there?"

****

For thousands of years, horseshoe crabs have come ashore to mate in late May during high tides on full moons. They gather in the shallows by the thousands, where males latch onto the backs of females. The females pull them up onto the beach, dig holes and deposit eggs in them. They then pull the males over the holes to fertilize them, before dragging them back into the water. When you see it done en masse, with a beach absolutely covered with them, it's quite a spectacle.

I first saw it 20 years ago while working on a magazine article about the overfishing of horseshoe crabs ('fishing' for horseshoe crabs means scooping them off the beach and tossing them into a truck). Daisy and I had driven down to Delaware through the night and, in the morning, walked onto one of the main horseshoe crab landing spots. We were a couple of days early but a handful of pairs were already fighting their way up through the surf. I sprawled out on the sand to photograph them tumbling through the waves, and as I did, four fishermen pulled up in a truck, looked around at the sparse pickings and drove off.

Later that morning, Daisy and I walked into a diner for breakfast, and the four fishermen were there. One of them recognized me from the beach and asked what I had been doing.

"Good Lord," he said, shaking his head when I told him, "horseshoe crabs are doing just fine."

I told him that studies of their populations had found otherwise. I also pointed to the black and white photos lining the walls of the diner. Each of them showed beaches packed with mountains of horseshoe crabs – multitudes more than could be seen today.

He was still unimpressed. "Horseshoe crabs aren't going anywhere. They've been around since the dinosaurs."

One of his friends put a hand on his arm. "Seen any dinosaurs around here lately?"

In the years since, the situation has only grown worse. But the beach migration is still something to be seen. And my hope today was to see the horseshoe crabs underwater, massed in the shallows before they marched up the beach.

Originally, I was going to drive down by myself. The night before, though, my 16-year-old son Zeke had blown off his curfew, turned off his cell phone and come home hours after he was supposed to. I took it as a cry for help – his way of saying he needed more Dad-time.

So at five o'clock the next morning, only an hour after he had dragged himself home, I dragged him back out of bed for the seven-hour drive to Delaware. He was not happy and we spent the first 45 minutes in stony silence. After a donut stop, though, the ice thawed and the rest of the drive went fine.

Sometime around noon, we stepped onto Pickering Beach in Dover. Once again, due to scheduling difficulties, we were a few days ahead of the full moon. But there would still be plenty of horseshoe crabs – the horny ones who couldn't wait.

The tide was out and signs of the early migration

were all around us. Hundreds of horseshoe crabs, upended in the surf and unable to right themselves, had been left to die on the beach when the tide went out. It couldn't have been an easy death. The sun was beating down and the humidity was brutal.

I looked at the water, brown and muddy, and the small glimmer of hope I had had of seeing the horseshoe crabs underwater faded. But I had come too far not to even try so I pulled on my wetsuit and headed in with a mask.

I've walked 50 feet straight out from the beach but I'm still only in up to my knees. The water is so muddy that I can't see my feet. I take a step and my right foot touches what is clearly a horseshoe crab. I take a step with my left and feel another. And then another with my right. Soon they're so thick that I can't put my feet anywhere.

I ease down into the water and my wetsuit keeps me afloat on the surface, inches above the blanket of invisible horseshoe crabs. I put on my mask and look down but I can't see anything. I can feel them, though, everywhere, pressed in together, their shells hard and sharp. Using just my hands, I scull over them, reaching down lightly to touch their shells now and then.

One hundred and fifty feet from the beach, the feel of their numbers starts to drop off. Two hundred and fifty feet from the beach, I feel only stragglers – those still heading in or those that have already mated and are headed back out. Three hundred feet from the beach, they're virtually non-existent. Even here, though, visibility is zero. But I can finally stand without fear of stepping on them.

I look back at Zeke on the beach and the stretch of water between us, knowing that it's jam-packed with horseshoe crabs. Reluctantly, I lie down on the water again and scull back in, passing just over the mass of unseen life until I'm close enough to stand up.

Zeke and I still had a few hours to kill before the horseshoe crabs would come out at high tide. But if there was anything to do for entertainment, I didn't see it. So when he suggested we take a walk up the beach, I agreed.

I realized quickly, though, that 'us' taking a walk up the beach meant him walking 30 yards ahead so no one would know we were together – even though there was almost no one else there.

I stopped to look at one dead horseshoe crab on the sand. It was big and its eyes were insect-like. Horseshoe crabs actually have ten eyes scattered over their bodies, including one on their tail and five on their undersides.

Technically, horseshoe crabs aren't really crabs. They're more closely related to spiders. And one look at their purplish undersides – especially when they're upside-down and their legs are moving in unison – makes that very clear. They also have little edible meat on them, which begs the question of why they're fished in the first place. Most are chopped up and used for fertilizer. Others are drained of a portion of their blue blood, which is used in medical research. Pretty much every flu shot you've ever taken was possible because of research done with horseshoe crab blood.

Zeke stopped and bent over a horseshoe crab up ahead. "Hey, Dad," he yelled, "I think this one's still alive."

"I doubt it," I said. "It's too hot."

He stared down at it. "I think it is."

I walked up and took a look. Indeed, the horseshoe crab's legs were moving slowly in unison, trying to gain some traction in the air. Zeke flipped it over and it turned toward the water and headed that way.

"Here's another one," he said a minute later.

I looked at the horseshoe crabs scattered around us and realized that only about half of them were dead. The other half were not moving but their spike-like tails – their telsons – were pressing down, arching their bodies up off the sand, trying to right themselves. We started flipping these crabs over and they immediately turned and headed for the water, too. I flipped over a few limp ones just to be sure, but they were dead.

Zeke and I kept walking up the beach, flipping over every crab we could see was alive. I looked down at one pair, a male and a female upside down, still clasped together, their legs limp and covered with sand. They had struggled up the beach, been flipped over, and left in the sun for what must have been a protracted death. And yet they never let go of each other. Maybe it isn't true that we have to die alone.

"How long do you think they can survive on land?" Zeke asked.

"I have no idea," I said. "A day. Maybe two. I guess the hotter it is, the quicker they die."

We reached the end of the beach, turned and

walked back. All along the way, the crabs we had flipped over had left tractor-like trails in the sand leading straight to the ocean. Most had already disappeared into it. As we walked, we flipped over a few we had missed, then watched them crawl to the water.

We made it back to where we had started, about halfway down the beach. A path there led back to our car. The sun was beating down, the humidity still draining. I could see dozens of horseshoe crabs on their backs on the half of the beach we hadn't covered but I didn't say anything. I knew Zeke was hungry.

"We should just keep going," he said. "There are a lot more crabs up this way."

And just like that, any concerns I had about him turning off his cell phone and blowing off his curfew disappeared. Any teenager who could put the lives of a bunch of overturned horseshoe crabs above his own need for food was okay with me. More than okay.

We continued down the beach, sometimes walking together, sometimes apart, flipping over horseshoe crabs we could see were alive. I passed one that was tangled in fishing line, held upside-down to the stump of an old piling. It was covered with sand and gravel and flies. There was no way it was alive.

I kept walking but a minute later, Zeke called out. "Look at this one, Dad. It's kind of tied to a stump."

"Yeah, I saw it. I'm pretty sure it's dead."

"I don't think so."

I walked back and looked down. The horseshoe crab's legs were so tangled that none of them could move.

"Even if it isn't dead," I said, "I don't know how we could get all that line away without ripping its legs off."

Zeke pulled out his pocketknife. "I can do it." He began to cut carefully, piece by piece, moving sand and seaweed out of the way as he went. Five minutes later, he had cleared enough for the horseshoe crab to move its legs. Ten minutes later, the crab was free. Zeke set it down on the beach and it began a slow march to the water, only ten feet away. It made it into the shallows then stopped, the top of its shell still breaking the surface.

"Do you think it's going to be okay?" Zeke asked.

"I couldn't tell you," I said. "But even if it isn't, dying in the water has to be better than dying upside-down in the sun."

The tide was now pushing in and nearing high. Small waves, brown with mud, began building and breaking on the beach. At first, there was no sign of the horseshoe crabs I knew were there. Then two telsons pinwheeled through a wave as a pair of them fought to get ashore. Then there was another pair. Soon, dozens of pairs of horseshoe crabs were tumbling through the waves, latched together, landing upside-down, getting hit by the next wave, being swept up and tossed forward again. Some pairs would land upright and hit the sand walking until they were clear of the surf. Other pairs would still be on their backs or their sides. Some pairs would be pulled apart. Even in these small waves, the struggle looked enormous.

Those that made it, continued up the beach. When they were done, they turned back to the water, fighting their way through the waves again, past others still battling to come in.

It looked nothing like the old black and white photos in the diner. There were a few dozen pairs but, as I said, we were early. When I finished photographing them, we walked back to the car and I programmed the GPS for our next stop – visiting family in Philadelphia. As I did, Zeke stared straight ahead.

"That was really cool," he finally said.

****

I walked into Bobby's new hospital room not knowing what to expect. I had visited him three more times at the rehab center and each time he seemed to be stronger. Then his condition plummeted and he had to be transferred to this hospital.

The room was as high-tech and sterile as any I had ever seen. His older daughter was already there. I tried to talk to him about the diving in Maine and the horseshoe crabs in Delaware but he was heavily drugged and drifted in and out of consciousness. There were no silent monologues. There was no writing. There were just the beeps and whirs of the machines he was hooked up to.

He grew more alert when his nurse walked in. She checked his vitals, then asked if he were in pain. He nodded yes. She asked him to rate it on a scale of one to ten. Over the years, I had seen nurses ask him this many times. He always answered with a 'five' or a 'six.'

Not today. He raised both hands and held up all ten fingers.

Four days later, Bobby's daughter messaged me that he had asked to be taken off the ventilator and had died peacefully. I went for a long walk, then dug out the 35mm slides I had shot in his class all those years ago. I was glad he was out of pain. I was glad he was out of that wheelchair. But I missed him already.

****

The woman behind the motel reception desk squinted at my shirt. "Massachusetts Institute of Technology Scuba Club." She looked from it to me, trying to figure out if I really was *wicked smaht*.

I did not, in fact, go to MIT. But I gave a talk there once and, in return, they gave me the shirt.

"I bet you're here to dive the bridge," she said, her southern accent strong.

"Yes, I am."

She smiled and nodded, turning back to her computer. "I knew it. People come from all over the world to dive that bridge."

She handed me a room key. "Now, have you ever dived the bridge before, darlin'?"

"I have."

"That's great. And you have friends here to dive with?"

"I do."

"Well, that's very nice. I hope you have a wonderful time."

The next morning, I pulled into the parking lot beside the Blue Heron Bridge in Riviera Beach, Florida. The bridge covers the small beach here, making it one of the few you can go to to get *out* of the sun.

As world-class dives go, it's a strange one. There's no reef. There are no big shipwrecks. Even at high tide, depths are generally less than 20 feet. But the turquoise bay is separated from the ocean by a slice of land, with one inlet feeding into it, so marine life streams in with the tides, then has trouble finding its way back out. The whole area is kind of a giant ocean aquarium. Currents are strong so the beach can only be dived at high slack – but that slack lasts close to three hours.

I walked under the bridge's shadow while a trio of toddlers wobbled about on the sand, their families watching from blankets spread out a few feet away. Two fishermen were casting from the concrete footing of one of the bridge's supports. A group of homeless men were gathered at one of the many picnic tables set out between the palm trees.

"Jerry, I've been looking all over for you!"

I turned and saw Sandra Edwards coming toward me, tall and thin, her red hair braided into two long pig-tails. Sandra, a New York transplant, was the first un-derwater photographer I had ever met who would find something, point it out to me, then back away so I could shoot it first. Most photographers will only get your at-tention after they've taken their own shots. Many will let you swim by without saying anything. A few will try to hide what they're shooting.

"Are you ready to head in?" Sandra asked. I knew

From the surface, you would never know that the Blue Heron Bridge is one of the world's great dives.

she was planning a marathon bike workout after the dive and didn't have time to waste.

"I have to wait for Ariane," I said. "She's bringing me some gear."

"Great. She just called and she's on her way."

A few minutes later, Ariane Dimitris pulled into the lot, too. I had met Ariane a few years earlier when she emailed me some questions about northeast nudibranchs, and then came up to Massachusetts a few weeks later to see them for herself. Fifteen minutes into that dive, I saw her shaking with cold. This will be a quick one, I thought. But an hour-plus later, it was me telling her that it was time to get out.

Ariane had brought a wetsuit, BC, tank and weights for me to dive with, saving me the hassle of having to pack them. They all fit perfectly.

While we geared up, Ariane described a long list of impossibly tiny creatures she had found here on her last dive – she has the eyes of an underwater eagle. As she talked, three guys pulled in, parked beside us and started gearing up, too. Many sidelong glances started going Ariane's way. The guys then made a few attempts at conversation. But she was engrossed in the minutiae of the minutiae and noticed none of it.

When we were ready, we found Sandra at the water's edge and headed in.

The white sand and rubble bottom is almost perfectly flat. Sunlight is rippling over it, with clusters of seaweed pushing up here and there like little patches of crabgrass. The water is 81 degrees and the current is still easing in. I'm inching along between Sandra and Ariane but see nothing of interest. Neither do they.

For ten minutes, we move at a snail's pace, poking and prodding the sand. I'm not wearing quite enough weight and every time I stop moving, I float up toward the surface and have to kick a bit to get back down.

Finally, I pass over a trio of fireworms – each two inches long with an orange head and brilliant white bristles lining the sides of its body. These worms are beautiful but divers here consider them little more than a nuisance. The white bristles are venomous – designed to break off inside the mouths of predators. I once saw a boy standing in waist-deep water hold one out to Sandra and ask what it was. Her eyes widened and she knocked it from his hand, saving him a painful sting.

As the fireworms tangle over one another, Sandra lets out a high-pitched yodel. I have no idea how she makes this noise but it's a great way to get someone's attention. She points at the bottom but I see only rubble. Her finger moves in closer and a small fish, an inch long and blending in so well as to be almost invisible, materializes. It's a lancer dragonet. But Sandra's finger is still pointing, moving back and forth. There's another one beside it.

These little fish are known for their mating rituals. At night, males dart up off the bottom, flaring their dorsal fins to attract females. Those that succeed in attracting a partner swim side-by-side with their prospective mates, wriggling and then mating in the water column. If another male sees them, though, he may try to push the first male's dorsal fin down, making him less appealing. He might even pretend to be a female himself and *faux* mate with the first male to confuse the female into swimming off. Sandra continues pointing to make sure I've seen them both, then backs off, giving me room to photograph them first.

Ariane is now yodeling, too, pointing at a nudibranch moving across the sand. It looks less than an eighth-of-an-inch in length. How she saw it I don't know. Sandra yodels again, louder and more insistent. She points at what looks like an underwater grasshopper. It's a sacoglossan – the vegetarian version of a nudibranch. I can tell she's excited about it, but even still, as she points, she sculls backward and waves me in.

Sandra and Ariane are now making one find after another: sea horses, multiple species of shrimp, blennies, more nudibranchs. Ariane has an underwater slate and she writes the name of each on it but I forget them all immediately.

We find a magnificent urchin (that's its name) moving across the sand. Its six-inch spines are a mix of red and yellow and orange and they radiate out in clusters between lines of iridescent blue spots on its body.

We've been underwater an hour and I finally find something on my own. It looks like a coconut cut in half, with stiff porcupine-like spines growing off it. I'm not sure if I'm looking at an animal or the leftovers from someone's picnic. Sandra's focused on something else but when she looks up, I wave to get her attention. I really need to learn that yodeling thing.

Sandra looks at it and nods excitedly. I find out later that it's a coconut urchin – a creature rarely seen because it spends most of its life buried under the sand. At last, I get the chance to back off and wave Sandra in for the first shots.

Ariane yodels. Her face is pressed to the back of her camera, not looking away from whatever inconceivably small and camouflaged thing she's found. I swim over and stare at the square inch of sand in front of her camera port. I see nothing. Without looking up, she waves her hand and points at a beer bottle beside her. It's encrusted with coral, and empty shells are scattered around the opening. It's an octopus den, and the empty shells are the leftovers from past meals.

I peek inside without touching it. Lines of suction cups are squeezed within, filling the bottle. It's hard to imagine how the octopus fit through the opening. But I doubt there's any other creature on Earth with a body so malleable.

I move away and immediately find a second octopus squeezed into a small hole. And then I find a third under a tire buried in the sand. This happens all the time – as soon as you see one of something, you start seeing it everywhere.

Within minutes, I've found a half-dozen more, all in their dens. Finally, I see one out in the open. It's pulling itself along the bottom, arms stretching and reaching ahead, grabbing rocks, touching bottles, probing holes. Every few seconds it changes direction. It pauses, looks at me, then continues on.

Its body is a piece of inspired engineering. It can flatten, compress, or re-shape itself. It can change color completely in a microsecond to blend in – even though it's almost certainly color blind. Its arms are equipped with powerful suckers, each with senses of feel and chemical smell beyond anything we can imagine. In an emergency, it can drop any of these arms – and then regenerate them.

Its brain – along with squid and cuttlefish, its close relatives – is the largest of any invertebrate in the world. And it uses that brain well. Accounts of captive octopus working through mazes, solving puzzles, opening jars to get to food inside, have become commonplace. So have stories of them escaping from one tank, slithering across rooms and climbing into other tanks full of fish (i.e., dinner), and then returning to their own, unnoticed except by security cameras. Over and over, we see octopus demonstrate the ability to not only think but to plan.

I try to stay back from this octopus but it finds a crevice and slides into it, its body squeezing, bulging, then compressing and disappearing.

Where I've stopped, a mantis shrimp is pushing sand and rocks up through the entrance to its hole. I settle in to watch. As I do, ten feet away, the octopus slides halfway out of the crevice, sees me, then squeezes back into it.

I start to swim off but stop in front of a small gray fish standing straight up in a hole, its pectoral fin flared out behind it. It's a sailfin blenny and we stare at each other for a minute, until I notice something moving back where the octopus had been.

It takes a few seconds but I realize that it's the octopus' eyes – and just its eyes – rising up like a pair of periscopes. The rest of the octopus is still hidden. They look to the spot where I had been with the mantis shrimp. Then they swing around to the left, then around to the right. Then they rise up a bit more, come all the way around and look straight at me. I'm now eye-to-eye with a pair of eyes – until they sink back down into the hole.

Three hours after going in, we were back on the beach.

"Still want to make another dive somewhere else?" Ariane asked.

We had talked about a second dive but it was late in the afternoon, very hot, and the other site was an hour away. I didn't want to lose the good feeling I had.

"I'll just see you back here tomorrow," I said.

As I drove back to the motel, I saw Route 95 ahead

of me and thought, for the first time, about turning onto it and visiting to my father's old place a few exits down. It wasn't that my father and I had been close. We hadn't been. He and my mother had divorced when I was three and I could count the number of times I had seen him after that.

But one of those times stuck out. I was 12 – just a few months after my 'dive' at Flag Rock. He had shown up unexpectedly with a duffel bag full of masks, fins and snorkels – all of them black, all of them rubber. It turned out he was a diver and had heard that I wanted to be one, too. He disappeared again almost immediately but I treasured that gear.

Years later, after not having seen or heard from him for decades, I decided to track him down, let him know that he had a grandson and see if he wanted to take another crack at the family thing. It turned out he did.

After that, he called like clockwork every Sunday night. He and I would talk a little, then he'd get on the phone with Zeke for a while, and we'd repeat the process seven days later. It was nice.

At the same time, though, I had no illusions about him. He and I were different in almost every way. We had different ideas about what was important. We had different views of the world. Our politics were diametrically opposed. And I was glad for the differences.

One of those Sunday nights, though, we started talking about diving. It turned out he had given it up. Most of the people he dove with had either died or moved on. "I still have my gear, though, just sitting here," he said. "I should send it to you."

A few days later, a box arrived. I had no idea what

to expect. Most of my gear is not only old school but kind of unique. I didn't know anyone else who used any of it. I doubted I'd be able to use any of his.

I opened the box and couldn't believe my eyes. His gear and mine were the same. I mean, identical. He used the same make and model regulator, the same big, three-window mask and the same heavy fins. He and I were different in almost every way – except this. I wasn't sure what to make of it. I'm still not. He passed away soon afterward.

As 95 approached, I moved into the right lane to go up the ramp, but at the last second, kept going straight and passed it by. There just weren't enough memories there – not spread out over the course of a lifetime.

I pulled into the bridge parking lot at 10:30 the next morning. Before I was even out of the car, Anne Dupont – compact, buzzing with energy, her salt-and-pepper hair cut in a bob – was walking toward me quickly. "Jerry, I lied to you. I said we couldn't go in until 11 but Ariane and Sandra are already in and –"

She stopped herself and took a breath. "Hello, Jerry!" she said, raising her arms for a hug. Anne is one of the co-authors of the book *Sea Slugs of the Caribbean* and has an almost encyclopedic knowledge of the marine life here. "Okay, even though it's early, there's almost no current out there so we have to hurry to get in."

By 'we' she meant me. She was already in her wetsuit. Her tank and camera were already rigged and ready to go. She double-timed it back across the lot as I geared up, then pulled on her tank when I was ready.

"There aren't many grandmas doing this," she said with a happy cackle. "I'm going to take you to the Snorkel Trail first, then we can go wherever you want."

The Snorkel Trail was a new addition to the area – a line of underwater boulders just off the beach, large enough to act as a mini-reef and shallow enough for snorkelers to swim down to.

Anne held her hand to her eyes and looked out over the water. A dozen dive flags bobbed up and down on the surface off to the right, where we had been yesterday. "I think Sandra and Ariane are over there but ... well, we'll catch up with them sooner or later." She cackled again, then pulled on her mask and headed under.

We're moving along the sand, heading straight out from the beach. Brilliant sunlight dapples across the bottom. A stingray, six feet long from head to tail, glides by a few feet over the sand. A minute later, the Snorkel Trail comes into view. It's an underwater jetty about thirty feet long and six feet wide. The top is only six or seven feet below the surface. All along it, colorful fish – grunts, angelfish, butterflyfish, damselfish, chromis – are flitting about in flashes of yellow, purple and blue. Snorkelers, mostly kids, are dashing down from above, excited, arms and legs flailing.

On the offshore side of the boulders, Anne points into a 55-gallon drum cut in half and partially buried in the sand. I look inside. A porcupine fish – two feet long and heavy-bodied with large, expressive eyes – stares out at me nervously.

In ten minutes, we've circumnavigated the boulders and move away from them. Anne immediately adopts the same attitude as Sandra and Ariane yesterday – moving slowly, poring over every inch of sand, looking for life too small, too well camouflaged, or both, to be easily seen. She waves. A jelly – its bell eight inches wide and its short tentacles a forest of amber and blue – is lying on the bottom upside-down, pulsing. It's an upside-down jelly and this is how it's supposed to be. Even when it swims, it does so upside-down. The pulsing of its bell moves water through its tentacles, bringing in plankton to eat.

Its tentacles are also home to colonies of plant cells known as zooxanthellae, with whom the jelly has a symbiotic relationship. It provides them with a home and they provide it with extra food from photosynthesis. That's why the jelly is upside-down – to orient them toward the sun. The zooxanthellae have a similar relationship with coral and it's their death that causes coral bleaching.

Anne points into the jelly's tentacles. I see nothing – nothing but jelly, anyway. She points in closer. A pair of nudibranchs, each an inch long, is moving over the tentacles. They're a species that always makes its home in upside-down jellies. There's nothing symbiotic about this relationship, though. They are eating the jelly alive. And when there's nothing left of it, they'll set off across the sand in search of another one.

Anne waves me in to photograph the jelly and nudibranchs first, then moves in to shoot it herself. There is a problem, though. Because I was a little light and floating up in the water yesterday, I put an extra 4-pound lead weight – the lightest I could find – in the left pocket of Ariane's BC this morning. I'm now heavy enough to stay down but I'm listing significantly to the left and kicking extra hard with that leg to get back on an even keel. Every time I give one of those extra kicks, I send a plume of sand up into the water column. Each of those plumes seems to move horizontally through the water, stop directly over Anne, and then rain down on her. She pulls back from the jelly and looks up at the sand cloud that's only over her, then looks around, trying to figure out where it's coming from. I'm trying to look innocent but it's not easy when you're hanging in the water column rolled a half-turn to the left.

Anne moves back in and starts shooting again. Without thinking, I give another kick to right myself, sending more sand up into the water, then watch in horror as it drifts over to Anne and rains down on her again. She looks up, exasperated, then realizes it's all coming from me. She points emphatically at my fins and wags her finger. I'm being scolded by the diving grandma!

Immediately, I stop kicking and roll again a half-turn to the left. The sand settles and Anne points deeper into the jelly's tentacles. Egg strings from the nudibranchs are draped across them. Not only is the jelly a moveable feast, it's also an unwilling nursery.

As we move away from it, Anne gives me a series of hand signals. As with Bobby, I understand none of them. I raise my hands palms up and shake my head (see how clear my signals are). Anne goes through them again slowly. And again, I get nothing. She shrugs and swims off.

This turns out to be a pattern. Every few minutes, she gives me a whole new set. And each time, I draw a blank. I can't help but wonder what she's thinking: what a dumbass? how did I get stuck with this guy? no wonder he has to dive by himself so much?

In between hand signals, we pass a tiny jawfish pushing sand up and out of its hole and another one out in the open, moving across the bottom. Anne lifts an empty scallop shell and there's a crab seemingly attached to its underside, so well camouflaged that I can only see it when it moves. Anne finds more nudibranchs – some black, some yellow, one that looks like frosting on a child's birthday cake. A filefish hides in a clump of sargassum seaweed floating just under the surface. Octopuses (yes, octopuses is the plural) are everywhere. A one-eyed burrfish (probably hooked by a fisherman) angles itself in the water to keep its good eye toward me.

We're now back at the bridge, in front of one of the big supports. The current has picked up and Anne taps me on the shoulder and gives another series of hand signals. She's nothing if not an optimist. She holds up one hand in a stop position, makes a waving motion, then points a single finger straight up and rotates it in a circle.

I think I have this one: from our stopped position, we should each go around the opposite side of the support and meet at the other end. I nod enthusiastically. As I turn, though, I can't help but see the disappointment on Anne's face (she told me later she was signaling that the current had turned, visibility would soon get bad, and we should head back).

She follows, though. As at the Snorkel Trail, there

are reef fish everywhere – schools of colorful grunts, puff-erfish with pursed lips, flounder camouflaged against the sand, a scorpion fish. Anne points to an I-beam, half buried in the sand but with a small crevice under its bottom flange. Three different species of shrimp, side-by-side-by-side, peer out.

Indeed, the current is now pulling strongly through the bridge supports and we make our way back to the entry point, where the current dies off. We pop up to the surface and Anne looks around for Ariane's and Sandra's flags. No sooner have we surfaced than a woman walks toward us through the water cupping her hands.

"I see you here all the time," she says to Anne. "Can you tell me what this is?" She holds out a small crab with what look like feathers growing from its legs.

"That's a decorator crab," Anne says. "It finds things on the bottom and attaches them to its shell to blend in. Now, you show it to your friend –" she gestures toward a man hurrying through the water to see what she's holding, "then take a picture of it and give it to Jerry, here. He'll put it back where it belongs."

Dive flags are scattered all over the surface and, in the glare, Anne can't tell which, if any, belong to Ariane or Sandra. She goes back down but her bubbles don't stray far.

The woman hands me the crab and I take it under and put it down by an outcropping of basketball-sized rocks. It immediately pulls a feathery tunicate off of one and rubs it back and forth over a leg until it's attached.

Anne catches my attention and waves me over. She points at a clump of brown seaweed. I move in close to see what's hiding in it. But it's not seaweed. It's a frogfish with seaweed-like strings covering its body. It's one of the weirdest looking fish I've ever seen. Its head and tail are sharply upturned. Its pectoral fins have evolved into feet. Not feet-like. Feet. Right in front of me, it starts to walk, taking slow, windmilling steps across the sand.

It walks a few feet then stops and reverts back into a seemingly harmless clump of seaweed. Only its eyes give it away. But even they have a line running through them for disguise.

I'm lying on the sand beside it, waiting for it to walk again, but instead a small blob of something starts bobbing over its mouth, jigging up and down. I wait, hoping the frogfish will lurch up and eat it but then realize that the blob is part of the frogfish. It has what amounts to a fishing rod on top of its head, complete with bait – the blob. Most of the time the rod lies flat against its head. To hunt, though, it lowers the rod in front of its face and dangles the blob above its mouth. Fish that come in for a closer look end up as dinner.

Minutes pass and nothing is showing interest. The rod slowly folds back against the frogfish's head. I'm not a fisherman but I've seen plenty of them when they decide nothing is biting. And this looks a lot like that.

I swim off to find Anne. She points at a bottle encrusted with coral. A blenny, seemingly straight out of Dr. Seuss, pokes its head out to look at me.

We've been underwater almost three hours and are now back near the entry point, at another of the bridge supports. It's covered with algae and tiny invertebrates. We're shallow enough to stand up but Anne is searching the support's vertical face. She finds what she's looking for and points. It's another blenny – a male Molly Miller – poking its head out from a small burrow in the concrete. And like many male Molly Millers, it's flipped over, taking an upside-down view of the world. No one really knows why.

I stowed my gear and walked back to Anne's SUV. The hatchback was up and she, Sandra and Ariane were sitting on the back edge surrounded by bowls of watermelon, mangoes and cookies. Diving with Anne is an all-inclusive experience.

She slapped me on the shoulder. "Hey, you did pretty good with my hand signals."

"What?"

"Well, considering that we didn't go over them before the dive."

I had to laugh out loud, trying not to spit out any cookies in the process.

****

A sharp turn off the highway in Portsmouth, Rhode Island leads onto a bumpy dirt road, through some bushes and out to a small inlet called Gull Cove. It's a beautiful little place but there's no beach here, other than the dirt and gravel off to the side of the road when the tide is out.

It was early morning when I pulled in under a dark sky. Fifty yards up the road, three fishermen were casting from lawn chairs at the water's edge. In two other cars, coffee drinkers looked out over the water.

Minutes later, it began to pour – a torrential rain that pounded the roof of my car so loudly I couldn't hear the radio. It was impossible to see out the windshield. Through the passenger door window, I could see rain pummeling the surface of the water. I dropped the seat back, closed my eyes and settled in.

When the storm finally passed, hot, muggy air hung over the cove. I took my time gearing up, making sure there wasn't a second squall following behind, then headed in.

Visibility is a murky ten feet. A blanket of slipper snails, their shells an inch long and nestled together in groups of five and six, covers the steep slope. There are thousands of them, all dusted with a thin layer of brown silt.

There are a few splashes of color. Yellow sponges are scattered about – some are oval and just a few inches from end to end; others are three to four feet long and irregularly shaped. I pick up one the size of a football. It's squishy and weighs almost nothing.

These are boring sponges – sponges that over-grow hard objects, animate and inanimate, then bore into them chemically until there's nothing left of them but their shape.

At 25 feet, the slope levels off and the blanket of slipper snails disappears. The bottom is pure muck –

brown and feathery and almost weightless. Everything I do, from moving my hand to adjust my mask, to changing the direction I'm swimming in, sends clouds of it swirling up into the water column.

Spider crabs are scurrying over it, leaving trails of silt rising behind them. A whelk – its shell ten inches long – is laying an egg string into the muck that looks like a pale corrugated hose an inch in diameter and more than a foot in length.

I pass over a scallop, its upper and lower shells open an inch. Forty bright blue eyes peer out from the hair-like fringes inside. These eyes don't see as ours do but can detect changes in light and movement. When the scallop 'sees' me, it rises up from the bottom and swims off erratically, its shells clapping together. It settles back down five feet away. This ability to swim is a trade-off: its shell is light and ribbed to be hydrodynamic but offers little protection against crushing.

Something big and silver is moving through the water just beyond the edge of visibility. I move toward it and it disappears, then reappears. It's a school of scup, about 30 of them, all flattened, silver ovals about a foot long. I try to stay close but they disappear into the murk.

I move back onto the slope and settle down on the slipper snails, motionless. Within seconds, something tiny zips by me on the bottom. Then again. And again. Over and over, small things are zipping by in every direction – sideways, toward me, away from me.

It takes a minute for my eyes to adjust to the quick movements. Finally, I focus in on one. It's a small fish, about an inch long and brownish-gray with proportionately large pectoral fins. It's a seaboard goby and it sits on the bottom angled toward me, its head arched up. It zips forward a few inches, stops and spins sideways. A second later, it zips headfirst into a hole, then re-appears looking out.

Now that I've seen one, I'm starting to pick them out all over. There are at least 20 of them on the bottom in front of me, zipping in and out of little holes in the muck and the crevices between slipper snails and boring sponges. Two of them look at me from one hole, their heads angled together, their faces comically expressive.

More little things zip away along the bottom but these movements are different. Again, it takes a minute for my eyes to adjust. They're juvenile flounder, all less than an inch in length, all blending into the bottom. Tiny crabs of a species I've never seen before, dark and spotted, are mixed in between them, scurrying quickly from one hiding place to another. This whole area is a nursery for the young and the tiny to gather and grow.

I'm in seven feet of water, only feet from the shoreline, and the current is pulling toward a narrow channel that feeds out of the cove and then offshore. I let it take me for an easy ride over boring sponges, orange sponges and what look like tiny frilled anemones.

At the mouth of the channel, I kick up the slope a few feet to where I can stand up and look around. I'm about 50 yards from my car. I drop back down and head to the bottom of the slope where the current is less, and start kicking back. Little flashes of movement zip away from me the whole way.

****

It was 5am in Calais, Maine, at the border crossing between the U.S. and Canada. Except for me and the customs agent in the booth, the place was a foggy ghost town. "Please pull up and park at the office building ahead," he said. "Someone will be waiting for you inside."

Being stopped at the Canadian border is a regular thing for me. I cross several times a year and it always happens. Most people answer a few questions and drive on. But not me. Or, should I say, not the guy who wears a Boston Bruins hat every time he goes to Canada.

I did as told and walked into the office.

"Where is your destination in Canada?" the agent behind the counter asked, her French-Canadian accent strong.

"Deer Island."

"You will be taking the ferry from L'tete?"

"*Oui.*"

"And what is your purpose for coming to Canada?"

"To scuba dive."

Her face lit up. "Ah, you are a scuba diver. You know about Awslow, don't you?"

"Awslow?" I said.

"Yes, Awslow."

I shook my head, not understanding.

She turned to the agent at the other end of the counter. "Awslow," she said, making a circular motion with her finger.

He shrugged. "No idea."

Suddenly I realized what she was saying. "Old Sow!"

"Yes, Awslow," she repeated. "I need to look through your car."

Old Sow is the largest tidal whirlpool in the Western Hemisphere and it churns away like a giant maw, surrounded by dozens of smaller maws all turning in different directions, right off Deer Island Point. Old Sow is not a thing to be trifled with. I once made the mistake of diving Deer Island Point without knowing the area well. At slack water, I went under and headed down a steep slope covered with some of the densest marine life I had ever seen.

I was about 130 feet deep when I felt the first tug of the building current and I started to ascend immediately. But I hadn't counted on the current higher up being stronger. When I hit 80 feet, it was blasting, pulling me sideways along the slope while I tried to make headway up. At 60 feet, it began pushing *down* the slope rather than across it, making it almost impossible to swim up. I began pulling on boulders, fighting my way hand-over-hand. I can still hear myself breathing Darth Vader-like, knowing that every extra minute I took was another minute the current grew stronger. At 40 feet, it was ripping so forcefully I was pulling microwave-sized rocks out of the bottom as I went. At 20 feet, the bottom turned to gravel and I had to dig my hands into it for every bit of extra pull I could get to avoid being swept offshore. At last, I was shallow enough to stand up and the current died off.

I dragged myself up onto the beach, dropped to my knees and rolled over onto my tank, gasping for air. At that moment, I decided two things: first, I would never tell Daisy about this dive (I actually did but it took a few years.); second, I would never dive Deer Island Point again.

Since then, I've dived at Deer Island dozens of times but never at the Point. According to Joe George, though, I made two crucial mistakes on that dive. And today he was going to show me how to do it right.

The customs agent finished going through my gear and the rest of the car. She snapped the glove compartment closed and shut the door. "I have always wanted to scuba dive," she said, then turned and headed back to the office. "Enjoy your stay in Canada."

Deer Island lies just off the New Brunswick coast, a rocky chunk of land in the Bay of Fundy. The island's southern end narrows sharply at the Point, with Old Sow swirling away just beyond. But every bit of the island's shoreline – not just the Point – is in a state of near-perpetual movement, with whirlpools and eddies building, speeding up, fading away, changing direction and building again.

Most of the island's sparse population is congregated in a few outcroppings of houses, businesses and churches at its northern end. I drove off the ferry there and wove through them. As I did, the water, and the feel of it, was never far away. Neatly kept piers, docked fishing boats and lines of old weir poles appeared regularly through stands of tall pine trees.

When I reached the Point, Joe was already there with two friends, John Prendergast and Matt Towns. Matt's wife and two young daughters, Addison and Olivia, were there as well. As I pulled in, the girls were running up from the beach, carrying a sloshing pail

Old Sow, the largest tidal whirlpool in the Western Hemisphere, swirling away just off Deer Island Point.

between them. "Joe," they yelled in unison, "we made you some soup!"

Joe was halfway into his drysuit but he stopped to look in the pail. Seaweed and a few other unidentifiable objects floated around in a reddish mix. "Tomato basil," he yelled, "my favorite!"

The last time I had seen Joe with Addison and Olivia had been at a group dinner during the Sea Rovers show in Boston a few months back. Throughout the meal, the two girls had climbed on him like a jungle gym. At one point, Olivia made it to the top of his head. Anytime I talked to Matt, I could tell he was only listening with one ear, the other ear scanning for whatever outrage Addison and Olivia were planning for Joe next. At one point, he spun away from me in mid-sentence, eyes wide, and whispered emphatically, "No knives!"

Later, I looked over and saw Joe with his arms on either side of his plate, a fork gripped in one hand, a spoon in the other, his face set in a death stare looking straight ahead while the girls watched him open-mouthed and fascinated.

Then the death stare dropped. "So, that's how you eat your food in prison," he said.

Back at the Point, Joe pawed through the 'soup' with a plastic spoon the girls had also found on the beach. "Let's see," he said, holding up a clump of green seaweed, "here's the spinach." He picked out some red seaweed. "Here's the tomato." He reached in and spooned out an empty exoskeleton. "And here's the shrimp!"

Addison and Olivia could barely contain themselves: yes, yes, yes, all that good stuff was in there. "Just eat it!"

"Wait a second," Joe said, holding out the spoon with a black clump of something on it. "Here's an old piece of rubber!"

"Just eat it!" they yelled.

I walked back to my car and started gearing up. Over the next ten minutes, I caught snippets of Joe's running dialog with the girls.

"... and he ended up getting squished so I guess it was kind of a love story ..."

"... you know, astronauts are just scuba divers who are afraid of the water ..."

"... in about an hour, your dad's going to thank me for giving you all those donuts ..."

As we waited for slack water, I nodded down at the sandy beach below us. "That's where I went in the last time I dove here," I said to Joe. The water beyond the beach was boiling like river rapids and, farther out, I could actually hear Old Sow churning away like a huge spinning wheel.

"Yeah, that was your first mistake, eh," he said. "We never, ever go in there when we dive the Point. And you probably went in at low tide, right?"

"Yeah."

"That was your second mistake. We never, ever dive the Point at low tide."

Indeed, when we finally headed to the water, we took a narrow path that curved away from the beach, down into a small patch of sand encircled by pine trees and massive boulders. Of the four of us, I was the only one wearing a single tank. Joe was wearing two side-mounted tanks slung from his waist, one on each side. Matt and John were each wearing doubles. I felt a little naked.

We walked into the choppy water and Joe turned to me. "Wait till you see the fingers," he said, "you're going to love them!"

The bottom is sloping away gently. Dark, sharply cut rocks seemingly barren of life cover it. Visibility is 25 feet.

Fifty feet down, the slope steepens and suddenly explodes with color and life. Northern red anemones – orange and red and purple – are everywhere, interspersed with stalked tunicates, sponges and sea peaches.

There are more species of starfish in front of me right now than I've seen the entire year so far. Large purple sunstars stretch out their multitudes of arms across rocks. Spiny sunstars – bright red with round bodies and short stout arms – are buried deeper in. A lone winged sea star, looking like a Christmas cookie with a bright yellow body and thick, orange tipped arms, holds itself vertically onto the slope. There are small blood stars, some purple, some yellow and some red. Countless yellow tendrils of basket stars stretch up through other invertebrates to feed. There's so much life that I can barely see any of the rock beneath.

At 90 feet, Joe and I stop, while John and Matt keep going, disappearing into the gloom. The boulder below me – about the size of a large pickup truck – is completely covered with sea cucumbers, well over a hundred of them, dark brown and huddled together. They're aptly named, shaped like huge cucumbers with a circle of arms on one end that branch out arborescently into feathery tentacles.

I see what Joe meant by 'the fingers.' Ridges covered with life rise up ten feet and run down the slope parallel to one another. A 15-pound lobster stares out at me from a dark opening surrounded by northern reds. A few feet away, another 15-pounder watches from a hole obscured by a curtain of stalked tunicates. A few feet deeper, I see a little guy – a 10-pounder – ripping at a yellow sponge with huge claws covered with barnacles.

There's so much life in every direction that it's hard to focus on any one thing. It's almost too much.

At the bottom of one boulder, I move down to a dark hole – a perfect wolffish den. If a wolffish lives here, though, it doesn't seem to be home. I move right up to it and shine my lights in. I can feel Joe at my shoulder, his head right beside mine, looking into the hole, too. Why is he so close, though? We have the whole ocean here.

I turn to nudge him away – but the face at my shoulder is huge and blue and has a mouthful of jagged white teeth. That's not Joe! The wolffish and I stare at each other for a few moments, our faces inches apart, and then it squeezes past me into the hole, disappears and reappears facing out. It's looking at me blankly now, probably wondering what I was just doing.

I move sideways across the slope and set down on one of the few bare spots of rock. Suddenly I realize my shoulders are very tense, my senses alert for any signs of a building current. But I know this dive is going to be fine. I let out a breath, relax and turn back to the slope and the massive display of life on it.

When we popped up in the shallows, Matt and John were already onshore, working their way back up the path.

"I had some kind of bug in my regulator," Joe laughed. "A big one!"

"A bug – like an insect?"

"Yeah, it must have sneaked in there when I was gearing up. As soon as we went under, it crawled out of the regulator into my mouth!"

"What did you do?"

"I ate him. He was pretty crunchy."

Joe looked up at Matt and John trudging up the path, then looked back at me. "So, better than your last dive here, eh?"

Drift dives aren't my favorite. You go in while the current's still running a bit and let it sweep you along in a controlled way from point A to point B like an amusement park ride. Most divers like them. But if you want to stop to photograph something or get a good look at it, it's not so easy. And if you do stop – usually by grabbing something on the bottom – you quickly get separated from whomever you're with.

At a place like Deer Island, though, where the currents only allow you a short time in the water, you have to take every opportunity you get. And so we parked on the opposite side of the Point and headed in an hour ahead of low slack. Our plan was to stay shallow enough to follow the island's curve. That way the current would swing us around and deposit us on the beach at the Point, rather than pulling us offshore into Old Sow. It was just Joe, John and me. Matt was already heading back to the mainland with his family.

I'm facing into the current, holding onto a rock to anchor myself. Joe is beside me, holding on as well. I'm not sure where John is. Joe taps my arm. I can see he's smiling around his regulator. He lets go of the rock and waves as the current takes hold and pulls him backward into the gloom.

I let go, too, and the current pulls me feet-first

over the rocky slope. I kick now and then against it to slow the pace. The bottom is mostly bare rock. A wolf-fish peers out from under a boulder. I grab onto a rock in front of its den and flutter like a pennant in the wind. I let go and am swept up by the current again.

A cluster of starfish zips by and then another wolffish. But there's not much happening. How can one side of the Point be so covered with life, and this side, just a few hundred yards away, be almost barren?

I glance back over my shoulder and see the glow of Joe's and John's lights. They're getting dimmer, though, so I stop kicking against the current and let it race me backward to them. A minute later, we're in the shallows, moving along a sand bottom and into waist-deep water.

A pair of young girls, a little older than Matt's, stood on the beach staring at us wide-eyed as we came up out of the water.

"How did we end up here?" Joe said loudly. "Hey, have you seen our boat?"

"There's a boat over there," one of the girls said, pointing to a ship far out on the horizon.

"Nope, that's not it," Joe laughed. "I think the guys on our boat must have left us here, you know, like in *Pirates of the Caribbean.*"

"No, they didn't," the other girl laughed.

Both started angling toward Joe, having already identified him as the one with whom they could best communicate. "Is it fun to be a scuba diver?" one of them asked.

"Is it fun to be a scuba diver?" Joe said. "Well, let

me tell you ..."

Low slack, and the next dive, was less than 20 minutes away but Joe and John hustled to stow their gear and catch the next ferry off the island. A couple of hugs later, they were gone. And just like that, as it usually does anytime Joe leaves a place, it felt very quiet. I saw no one else – not the two little girls, not their families, not anyone. The island's tourist season was still a couple of weeks off and its year-round residents were all congregated at its other end.

I considered rushing to catch the next ferry, too. Instead, I drove down the shoreline a short way to the beach where I usually dive. I walked down it and looked out over the water as the eddies and whirlpools churning its surface began to calm. And as I did, I couldn't help but wonder what was happening under there right at that moment.

I walked back to my car, popped the trunk and started gearing up.

Summer

I stood on a boat ramp in Jamestown, Rhode Island looking out over Narragansett Bay from Fort Wetherill. It was a beautiful afternoon and the former military base was crowded with picnickers, volleyball players, runners, swimmers, dog walkers. A flotilla of sailboats cruised off-shore, their spinnakers ballooning out in front of them. Fishermen were casting from the rocks, while seven different dive flags moved across the water in front of me.

This site is the most popular shore dive in Rhode Island, although that has more to do with free parking and easy entries than with the dive itself. The two coves here are mucky and exposed and visibility is rarely good. But I was looking for a warm, easy dive and this one fit the bill.

I'm 20 feet deep and have just opened the chest zipper of my wetsuit. Water floods in. My suit's too warm for Rhode Island – the water is 64 degrees – and the sudden inflow is a relief. As expected, visibility is terrible – five feet, perhaps – and sunlight is glaring through it, making it even worse.

A trio of rudderfish – two feet long and with bluish-silver bodies – swims in close then maneuvers around behind my head. I turn to face them but they turn with me, staying at my back. I stop and turn the other way but they change direction, too, then speed off into the bright murk.

I'm hoping visibility will improve away from the beach, when the rudderfish zip in again and maneuver behind me. They're within inches of the back of my head. I turn toward them and they turn with me. I change direction and they do, too. I turn around as fast as I can and they zip off.

A minute later, they're at the back of my head again with three other fish, also blueish-silver but only a foot in length. I can't turn around fast enough to see if they're juvenile rudderfish or a different species altogether. They zip off again.

I don't want to put up with this any more. I take a hard right, changing course 90 degrees, and head toward the far wall of the cove, kicking hard and moving fast to lose them.

Thin mud strings, two to three inches long, are hanging vertically in the water column everywhere. Hundreds of them. I reach the far side of the cove. The water is only 12 feet deep and a granite wall rises straight up from the sandy muck to the surface and beyond. Above the surface, leafy bushes lean out over the water. Long fronds of kelp drape down from just below the surface, swaying in the current. Small cunner and large tautog are all around. The cunner pay me no attention. The tautog, though, see me and swim off nervously, one after another.

At the base of the wall, a dead crab lies on its back

with a swarm of cunner feasting on it. Sand and muck is being kicked up in the excitement, and visibility here is less than a foot. I move in close and the cunner all back away, probably thinking I want some of the crab, too, then swarm back around me onto it.

I decide to cut across the cove to the wall on the opposite side on the off-chance that visibility is better there. Over the center of the cove, schools of scup are circling in the water column and dozens of small black sea bass are hanging by the bottom.

Other fish stand out in the murky water. A pair of butterflyfish – small ovals banded with black and yellow stripes – appear over a rock. A scrawled filefish, its long yellow body marked with iridescent blue lines, swims quickly away from me, while a pair of pufferfish, their bodies bloated and their lips pursed, set down on the sand to watch. All of these colorful fish are hundreds, if not thousands, of miles from their tropical homes.

The Gulf Stream, powering warm, blue water up the east coast, carried them on an unwilling journey north before spinning them out here. Through the summer and fall, they'll flit about, gaudy strangers in a strange land. But once winter comes, temperatures will drop and they will all die, unable to adapt and not programmed to migrate.

I reach the wall on the other side of the cove. Visibility is just as bad here. I unzip my suit again and let in another rush of water, then start back along the sand toward the beach.

****

When Daisy and I met, she didn't dive. But I'd take her to Walden Pond and stand in the shallows with my mask on. "Look at that," I'd say. Or, "There are so many fish here." After a few minutes, I'd take off the mask and put it on the blanket beside her. Eventually she picked it up.

"Look at that," I started hearing her say.

One courtship later, she signed up for a scuba class and we spent our honeymoon diving in the Caribbean.

Zeke was even easier. He wanted to dive as soon as he could walk. I'd tape string harnesses onto empty soda bottles and he'd run around the house with them pretending he was wreck diving. He also made regular tub dives, breathing through a regulator hooked up to a tank outside the tub while water splashed all over the bathroom. He was certified when he was ten.

Still, I tried not to push him. He and I made four or five dives a summer and that seemed like a good number. After a few years, though, he wanted to do it less and less. Skateboarding and surfing leapfrogged diving. But I didn't want him to completely give it up – not yet anyway – so I tried different things to keep him interested. And in Eastport, where we were for the week, that meant rooting around on the bottom for old bottles.

Daisy, Zeke and I, together with our dog Romi, pulled in and parked beside the old cannery. The sun was directly overhead, beating down with almost no shade anywhere.

I staked out a spot against the building to gear up and squeezed into the 18-inch shadow thrown from the eave high above. Zeke spread his equipment across a padded blanket behind the car. Daisy and Romi wandered off. We had to dive in two shifts because we couldn't trust Romi alone in our rented cabin. Left to his own devices in a strange place, he had an appetite for destruction. So Zeke and I would go in together first. When we came up, he and Daisy would switch.

Every few minutes, a car would drive past on the dirt road, sending clouds of dust up into the air. I poured a jug of water over my head to cool off, then pulled on my wetsuit. Zeke did the same.

At the water's edge, though, he gave me a forlorn look. "Do I really have to dive?"

"Nope."

He looked out over the water, then back up at the car, considering his options. "All right," he said, "but this is gonna suck."

And on that note, we headed in.

The current is still ebbing. It takes a hold of us at the bottom of the slope and carries us gently down the channel away from the wall, over muck and gravel littered with old skin cream jars, some white, some blue. Broken bottles of every shade of brown sweep by, along with other pieces of trash – the sole of an old boot, a blue rubber work glove, shards of plates and coffee cups.

Individual hydroids, bigger and more pendulous than those at Pierce Island, are also scattered over the bottom. Their heavy heads droop down like miniature sunflowers. We pass over an area marked by plastic yellow garden stakes driven into the bottom. We have a friend here who searches for bottles and marks out his areas like archaeological digs. When the current pulls us past the last of the stakes, we set down.

Intact bottles are scattered all around on the hard-packed mud and gravel. Zeke picks them up one by one, examines them and tosses them away. He holds one out for my opinion. I know little about bottles, though. But this one has an interesting rectangular shape. There's no screw-top, which means it's at least somewhat old, and its sides are embossed with lettering. I nod and Zeke pushes it into his mesh bag.

As he moves off, I see another one that looks interesting. I pick it up and surreptitiously drop it close to him. He sees it, picks it up, studies it and drops it back down. He knows more about them than I do.

Ten minutes in, Zeke has checked out all of the bottles exposed on the bottom. It's time to start digging. He roots through his bag for the gardening claw he uses but it must still be back at the cabin. He picks up a big clam shell instead and starts to dig. Silty muck rises up into the water and, in moments, we're enveloped. Zeke stops digging and what's left of the current pulls the silt away. He scans the hole and pulls out two partially unearthed bottles, sending more silt up into the water. He waits for it to be pulled away too, then examines them. One gets tossed, the other goes into the bag.

This process repeats over and over. I don't get involved. If he were younger, I'd feign an interest. But at 16, any curiosity on my part will just drive him away. So I hover nearby, enveloped in silt.

Thirty minutes in, Zeke taps me on the arm. He's done. His bag is full but I don't think he's found anything that rocked his world. We start back. The current has died so we don't have to kick against it.

About halfway there, Zeke spots the conical bottom of a bottle mostly buried. The muck and gravel here is packed even tighter and there are more rocks mixed in. He tosses the clam shell and starts digging with his fingers. We're quickly enveloped in silt and there's no more current to pull it away.

I can't see anything except for an occasional glimpse of Zeke's gloved fingers scraping at the bottom. Then he pulls the bottle free. It's a beautiful aquamarine blue and close to a foot long. Its sides are thick and its bottom shaped like the end of a football. It's a torpedo bottle. It was made this way at least 100 years ago so that it would be shipped on its side. The liquid in it kept the cork moist.

We're still enveloped in silt but I can see Zeke looking the bottle over, turning it in his hands. And I can see the smile on his face around his regulator.

Daisy has one condition when we dive: as much sunlight as possible. It took me a little while to understand this. I'd bring her down 70 or 80 feet to some

Zeke's torpedo bottle, pulled up from the mud after about 100 years underwater.

beautifully wild ledge and she'd hate it. It would be dark and cold with no sunlight. The fifteenth or sixteenth time she said it to me, I finally got it.

Now we stay shallow.

She and Zeke have switched places and we're heading down the slope but we stop about halfway and swim to the corner of the wall. Yellow frilled anemones cover the granite blocks here, with vermilion-colored nudibranchs tucked in between them, feeding on smaller hydroids.

I'm moving sideways along the wall but Daisy is locked in place – floating 15 feet beneath the surface, her hands tucked between her back and her tank. I always move slowly to see as much as I can but Daisy moves even slower. A lot of times, she barely moves at all.

I stay close but wander a bit – below her, above her. I turn around and look at the vast emptiness out and away from the wall. A large lion's mane jelly is drifting by. Its bell isn't pulsing and even though there's almost no current, it's tumbling in what little there is. It angles down and in toward the wall and hits it, bouncing off and continuing on, drifting down faster now.

It knocks into a rock at the base of the wall, gets hung up for a second then slips free. If the jelly isn't dead, it's certainly close. The current drags it along the bottom and it gets tangled in a group of urchins. The bell is two feet long and what isn't tangled hits a northern red anemone that immediately closes over it and starts to pull it in. In seconds, two large crabs scurry over on top of it, ripping pieces of it free.

I drop down to get a closer look. Daisy's up on the wall within view. I look for a place to set down but something else right below Daisy catches my eye. It looks like two northern red anemones somehow fused together. I swim in close. It is a northern red attached to a rock on the bottom. But it has two heads – two separate mouths with two separate sets of tentacles surrounding them, all on one body. Some species of anemone reproduce by splitting in two. Not northern reds. I circle around this one trying to figure out what I'm missing. But I'm not missing anything. It's a two-headed anemone.

The next day, I drove to Gleason's Cove in Perry, the next town over from Eastport. The rolling grounds in front of the water were mowed and manicured and set up with a couple of picnic tables. But there was no one else around. Sunlight glistened over the water. Two old fishing boats hung on moorings just offshore. I had only dived here twice before and hadn't seen much of anything either time. But you never know. And every time you think you do, you find out you don't.

The bottom is a mix of muck and smooth stones. Visibility is terrible, about three feet. I see nothing but green murk.

I've only been under for ten minutes but I'm going to turn around and head in. As I'm about to, the water in front of me darkens. Suddenly the snout of a shark, its mouth open and teeth exposed, comes out of the gloom two feet away. Instantly, it veers left and all seven feet of it glide by close enough that I can see the fluttering of its gills and every scratch and scar along the side of its body. Its tail swishes and it's gone.

I'm not afraid of sharks but this one just scared the crap out of me. It was a porbeagle – kind of a scaled-down great white.

For the rest of the swim back through the murk, I keep imagining its big head materializing in front of me again.

Jasper Beach in Machiasport, an hour south of Eastport, is a half-mile stretch of loose stones, thousands of them rubbed smooth from years of rolling through surf. The stones angle steeply up from the water to the

The stark beauty of Jasper Beach with a fog bank rolling in.

top of the beach, framed between two densely pined points.

A fog bank was rolling in. It had already enveloped the small islands just outside the cove. In front of it, sunlight glistened on swells that seemed to materialize from nowhere. Soon the fog covered the swells, leaving only the sound of them rolling in, hitting the beach and then dragging back down through the stones.

In another minute, the fog swallowed me up, too. The stark beauty of the place suddenly felt very lonely. I had been diving with friends more than ever and my tolerance for being alone seemed to be waning. I wished that Daisy or Zeke had come. Or Ed or Joe. Or anyone, really.

In a few minutes, though, the fog thinned and I could see the swells rolling in, then the pine forests at the points of the beach, and then the islands offshore.

I geared up at my car and walked down to the water, the loose stones on the slope sliding out from under each step. I took an angled route across them, then made the long walk at the water's edge all the way to the left end of the beach, where a line of poles – tree trunks stripped of bark and branches – stood straight up in the water about 30 feet apart. They were old weir poles and once had nets strung between them to catch fish. Red and yellow lobster trap buoys dotted the surface straight out from the last pole. They marked the one rock ledge in the cove.

I walked into the water and swam out on the surface alongside the poles. From the beach, they looked thin and frail. Now they towered above me, white and solid, each having withstood years of winter storms.

With two poles to go, the bottom became too deep to see. I dropped down there.

Underwater, the pole is draped in thick swaths of seaweed – red and yellow and green. Ten feet down, the seaweed disappears and a few seconds later, I settle on a bottom of sand and loose stones. Here, the ghostly white of the pole is even more stark. I can see the next one ahead and the one behind. It's like an underwater *Blair Witch Project*.

I swim along the bottom past the last pole and the ledge comes into view. It rises straight off the bottom five feet, then flattens out like a plateau. Mustard-colored kelp covers its top and drapes its sides, cascading down onto the sand. I can only see a section of it before it disappears into the gloom but I know from previous dives that it's about half the size of a football field.

Something is making a *clacking* noise ahead. Two large hermit crabs, each in a moon snail shell about the size of my fist, one slightly larger than the other, are on the sand. The smaller one has a hold of the larger one's shell and is pulling it back and slamming it into its own, trying to evict it. The hermit in the larger shell is hunkered down inside, reaching out with just its claws, trying to pinch the other one and loosen its grip. I watch the *clacking* and pinching for a minute, then move on.

I push aside a handful of kelp draping down the side of the ledge. The rock underneath it is covered with tiny striped whelks, each a quarter-inch long. I push aside another handful and an ocean pout – eel-like, three-feet long and brownish-green with large eyes and blubbery lips – zips out over the sand, turns and curls up to face me. I settle down in front of it and it unfurls itself and swims slowly away along the base of the ledge, its body undulating side to side. It settles on the sand again, turns and curls up. I settle down in front of it and it unfurls and zips under one of the few boulders beside the ledge.

I peer into the gap between the sand and the boulder and the pout peers back out at me. I don't see many of these guys any more and would like to get a longer look at this one. I kick up to the top of the boulder and set down where it can't see me, hoping it will come back out.

A large crab is walking across the sand toward us, ambling this way and that, until it's about three feet in front of the boulder. The pout rockets out, grabs it in its mouth and swallows it down in two bites. The crab never knew what hit it. The pout turns, sees me and zips back under the boulder. The whole thing took about two seconds. And the pout won't be coming out again – not with its belly full.

I push off from the boulder to the top of the ledge and swim just above the kelp covering it. There are more whelks and snails on the fronds. Crabs scurry under when they see me. I cut back and head in toward the shore again.

At the beginning of the ledge, an empty vodka bottle is lying on the sand. I'm about to swim past it when I see that there's a crab inside, too big to fit back out. It must have gone in to molt, stayed while its new shell hardened, and then found itself stuck like a ship in a bottle. It's staring out at me, helpless.

The only way to get it out is to break the bottle. But the instinct against breaking glass – even here, 30 feet underwater – is a strong one. It will just end up as sea glass in a few years, though. I pick up the bottle, push aside some kelp and tap it against the corner of the ledge. It makes a sharp *clink* but the bottle doesn't break. And the crab isn't happy. It's holding tight to the bottom, braced for impact. I hit it again, harder. It makes a louder *clink* but still doesn't break. One last time I bring the bottle down as hard as I can and it shatters. The crab slides down the side of the ledge on a piece of glass like a snowboarder, then slips behind the kelp and disappears.

****

Two weeks later, I stood knee-deep in the water

at Assateague Beach in Virginia, holding the bowline of my kayak, watching swells offshore roll in fast, build into waves, then break powerfully in the shallows with a *THWOOOOOMP!*

Daisy, Zeke and I had been spending a week at this beach every summer for years. No one ever dives here – the sand and waves and wash all combine to make visibility underwater close to zero. But I always wondered what would happen if I spent some time offshore, out beyond the waves.

It was still early in the morning and only a handful of people were in the warm water, ducking under waves as they broke. Two skim boarders stood higher up on the beach, timing the wash and waiting to hydroplane over the wet sand.

A bit farther out, beyond the surf, a woman, probably in her twenties, and an older man, probably her father, sat on surfboards, talking and rolling easily over the swells. The woman drifted away from the man, then paddled hard to catch an oncoming wave. She popped up and rode in front of it before slashing up its face and bouncing off, slashing up again and bouncing forward before riding it into the shallows, driving and pushing the whole way. She hopped off in the foam, then dove back onto the board and headed out again.

The man took his wave without even paddling, turning just as it built and letting it sweep him up. He rose into a low squat with his fingers lightly touching the sides of the board and stayed that way until it seemed he wasn't going to stand at all. But he did and then took a long, casual ride almost all the way up onto the beach. He stepped off with the same calm and paddled back out.

The two came together again out past the break, smiling, the woman using her hand to re-trace the line of her ride. Then they drifted apart to catch another one.

But the same waves they were having so much fun with, were bedeviling me. I didn't want to lose control of my 15-foot kayak in the surf and have it slam into some innocent bystander. Even here in knee-deep water, the force of the waves was almost ripping it from my hand.

At last I saw a break. I rushed into the water, pulling the kayak behind me, then jumped in just as a wave started lifting the bow and corkscrewing it sideways. I fumbled with the paddle, got a grip and dug in as hard as I could, paddling, straightening out and making headway over the wave. I punched through the next two and made it out past the break. The rest of the way, swells rocked the kayak up and down like a gentle see-saw until I was 100 yards offshore and the water calmed.

I turned and paddled an easy course parallel to the beach, still hearing the regular *THWOOOOOMP!* of the crashing waves. A trio of pelicans flew by, skimming just over the water in a line, barely flapping their wings and giving off a mellow vibe. A seagull sat on the surface farther out.

After a few minutes of easy paddling, I angled offshore again and paddled harder. As I did, a line of six dorsal fins began rollercoastering across the surface of the water 50 yards farther out. Dolphins.

When I was in my twenties, I worked as a mate and a captain on merchant ships and anytime dolphins appeared at the bow, I made an announcement on the PA. Within seconds, people – some of whom had been at sea their whole lives – would be lined up at the rails to watch them. The dolphins would torpedo along on the surface ahead of us, taking turns surfing the bow wave, their muscular bodies rippling. Sometimes an adult would nose a little one into the wave, teaching it to surf, too. I saw hundreds of them over that time. But I had never seen one underwater, face-to-face.

I didn't bother paddling toward this pod. They were moving too fast and it's against the law to approach them too closely. If they approach you, that's another story.

Over the next hour, I paddled a quarter-mile-square patch of ocean. Three more pods of what looked like bottlenose dolphins cruised by on the surface. None came closer than 30 feet.

I stop paddling. Minutes passed. Something splashed and a dark fish, a foot long, broke the surface and disappeared.

I looked back at the beach, 400 yards away. It was getting crowded with umbrellas and beach canopies. There were more people in the water, too. And the wind had picked up. I could hear the explosions of crashing waves.

The sun was starting to beat down. I put on my mask and slipped over the side. Even here, a quarter-mile offshore, visibility was only three feet. As I drifted, one arm slung over the top of the kayak, the surface of the water began to boil. A school of small fish had come to the surface all around me, with something bigger chasing them. And just like that, a pod of dolphins broke the surface ten feet away, their bodies glistening. They slid back under, broke the surface again and then disappeared.

I let go of the kayak and swam a wide loop around

it. The fish were gone and so were the dolphins. More minutes passed. I started treading water and swimming back and forth to the kayak.

More minutes passed.

Then the water started bubbling again, furiously this time, as if someone were taking handfuls of stones and throwing them across the surface. The bubbles started about ten feet away but within seconds were all around me. Hundreds of small, silver fish, each about an inch long, were dashing to the surface and then quickly swishing back down. I couldn't tell if they were the hunters or the hunted.

The bubbles headed away again and then started to fade. Fewer and fewer broke the surface. Then they were gone.

That's it, I thought, I'm heading in. And then a pair of dolphin fins broke the surface side by side 20 feet away and came straight at me. They disappeared underwater but a second later another pair took their place. Then they disappeared, too.

I pushed myself underwater, one hand reaching up and touching the bottom of the kayak, hoping to catch a glimpse of them. I saw nothing. But I could hear the clicks and squeaks so familiar from countless TV shows and movies.

And then a dolphin's face appeared at my side, inches away. It hovered in the yellowish water, drifting sideways around me so that it looked at me first with its left eye, then straight on with both, then with just its right. Its mouth was closed and set in the classic dolphin smile. We stared at each other for what seemed like minutes, although it was really just seconds, and then it was gone.

I pulled myself up and watched its fin cut along the surface, rollercoastering up and down and then disappearing. I looked around to see if there were others but that seemed to be it.

I pulled myself back into the kayak with a big dolphin-like smile on my face and started paddling in. With the swells at my stern, I was back in close to the beach in no time. Scores of people were now standing in the water, diving under crashing waves or bodysurfing on top of them. There seemed to be no place I could ride a wave in without coming dangerously close to someone – or a whole bunch of someones.

At last, I found a relatively unpopulated area and waited for a break in the waves. When the break came, I paddled into a five-footer. Instantly it lifted the kayak and kicked my speed up into warp drive. I paddled as hard as I could to maintain control, carving a course between two boys on boogie boards, aiming for thigh-deep water I could jump out into. A little girl in her father's arms watched me, grinning from ear to ear and cheering as I hurtled by.

****

North Carolina was in the midst of a drought – lawns were drying up and cars going unwashed. The drought was also having an effect on the beaches. Less rain meant less runoff. Less runoff meant saltier water close in to shore. And saltier water close to shore meant more sharks, which were being spotted off North Carolina beaches in record numbers.

I understood that this wasn't welcome news to everyone. But it was to me. I drove south through the night from Virginia, over bridges that stretched out over dark expanses of the Chesapeake, through tunnels that channeled under it, in and out of sleeping beach towns, until I pulled into an empty parking lot at Radio Island in Beaufort at four o'clock in the morning. Divers in North Carolina love this site for the small life that makes its home here. But I had a wide-angle lens on my camera.

The dark parking lot was ringed with brush and it wasn't obvious at first where the water even was. I had never dived here before. But I found a boardwalk and made my way down it, flashlight in hand. Up ahead, the beams of two other lights bobbed up and down, coming closer until two guys carrying the biggest fishing rods I had ever seen walked by with a wave. I took it as a good sign.

In another minute, the brush opened up to the water under a full moon. The tide was almost all the way in and the beach was just a narrow, curved strip of sand between the brush and the water. The jetty – the dive site – was all the way at the other end, a quarter-mile away. Small shapes scattered left and right as I walked – ghost crabs that only come out at night. And all around them, small, silver fish lay dead on the sand.

Halfway down the beach, I came to a couple hauling in a net. "Do you know what kind of fish those are?" I asked, pointing back to the dead fish on the sand.

"Most of them are spots," the man said. "A few might be mullet."

"They're not from us," the woman said. "I think those shark fishermen were using them for bait."

She must have meant the two guys with the fishing rods.

"Are you here to fish?" she asked.

"No, to dive."

"Oh, my brother-in-law dives here all the time," she said. "He has one of those little cameras you wear on your head. He gets great video of all the little fish down at the jetty."

I wished them well and started walking again. Minutes later, the beach came to an abrupt end, with the jetty continuing out into the water parallel to the land rather than perpendicular to it. Moonlight played across the inlet and the air was pleasingly humid. To the east, the dark sky was just starting to redden.

I hustled back to my car, taking a shortcut through the dark brush, eager to get in the water and, as Jimi Hendrix once said, watch the sunrise from the bottom of the sea.

A bit of moonlight is streaming down, enough that the sand isn't completely dark. It's moon-dappled. It's never easy to estimate visibility at night – I can only see what's in my lights – but it isn't good. The water, though, is as soft as any I've ever felt.

My lights hit the boulders of the jetty, splotched with sponges. Tucked in between two of them, a black sea bass lies on its belly sleeping. In front of another, a little sea robin wriggles and covers itself with sand.

I keep moving through the darkness but can't help thinking that this is where everyone dives. If I want to see something different, something bigger, I need to dive it differently. I need to be back along the slope where the shark fishermen were. I turn and head that way.

Just like that, I'm alone. There are no fish or crabs anywhere. For long minutes, I swim without seeing anything but rubble in my lights, as the water slowly changes from black to dull gray. It's twilight, the in-between time when the ocean's night shift has gone into hiding and the day shift hasn't come out yet.

And then in an instant the water is bright as day. The sun is up. A pair of juvenile black sea bass appear and swim in for a closer look, zipping back and forth and in and out like hummingbirds, while a third hangs back in the water column. A juvenile sea robin, an inch long, walks on its 'fingers' over the sand and rubble and broken shells until we're face-to-face, then spreads its pectorals wide. It's identical to sea robins farther north but the blue spots on its fins seem more iridescent, more tropical. It turns to walk away, but when I start to swim off, it turns and follows me. I turn back and it walks away again. I turn to swim away and it follows again. It wants whatever my fins might kick up but it's not interested in being the center of attention.

Four spadefish – silver with dark stripes and almost triangular because their dorsal and ventral fins are set so far back on their bodies – swim in, then speed up and scoot away. A lone sheepshead – colored just like the spadefish but with a more traditional shape – comes alongside and stays with me for a minute before swimming straight up the slope and disappearing. A pair of butterflyfish – yellow and white ovals – flit around a foot-ball-sized rock set into the slope. Each has a dark spot near the rear of its body. The spots look like eyes and con-fused predators can't tell head from tail or the direction they're going to swim in.

These fish are the only color in sight. Everything else is gray or tan or white.

I pass over a scrum of blue crabs and they scurry away sideways in every direction. One pair doesn't move – a large male cradling a smaller female in his claws. Crabs can't mate through their shells, so a male will carry a female that's close to molting everywhere he goes to make sure he's there in the brief window between her old shell being discarded and her new shell hardening.

I head out into the channel and visibility is even worse here. Sand dollars are scattered all about. A pur-ple starfish is moving surprisingly fast over the bottom. And another school of spadefish swings in for a look then speeds off. Other than that, there's little happening.

I head up the slope and pop to the surface. I'm only halfway down the beach. I can't believe that. I've been underwater almost two hours. But the shortcut through the brush is right in front of me. I'll get out here.

The sun is now well up. I'm done underwater but not ready to come out yet. I lay back and float on the sur-face, watching seagulls fly overhead, listening to them caw. The water still feels impossibly soft and I close my eyes. I've never been in an immersion tank but I can't believe it would be more relaxing than this.

I didn't take a single photograph during the dive, coming up as empty as those shark fishermen. But the water feels too good to be disappointed.

****

"Is that a striped bass?" I asked, looking down at the dark water. Whatever it was, it was moving slowly – possibly swimming – along the bottom through the shallows. But then it folded almost in half lengthwise and I figured it was a loose piece of kelp. Noe Lazo – solid and tanned, his black hair just starting to show some gray – stood on the other side of me, waist-deep, pulling on his fins and paying no attention.

I was back in Rockport, Massachusetts for my first full night dive of the year, which made it ideal for Noe. He seems to only dive at night. He's like a deep-sea fish whose eyes have evolved to see in the darkness. We once made a dive where his light died ten minutes in. It didn't matter. He made the dive in the dark with the little bit of moonlight coming down from above and the glow from my own lights beside him.

It was 10pm and the lights of Bearskin Neck shimmered over the bay, sending long reflections across the water between us.

When my fins were on, I took another look down at the 'piece of kelp'. It was now inches below the surface and slithering through the water. I turned on my lights and hit it full-beam. It was an American eel – green and two feet long. I had never seen one in the ocean before.

American eels are born in the ocean but quickly migrate into freshwater rivers and lakes. They live there

The lights of Bearskin Neck reflecting across the bay. You can see them underwater as diffuse bands of light.

until they're about five, then migrate back out to the ocean and swim all the way down the east coast to the Sargasso Sea, just east of the Bahamas, for a mass spawning. After that, they die. But currents sweep their larvae back up the coast until they hatch, migrate into rivers and lakes and the cycle begins again.

Most fish can't switch back and forth between salt water and fresh. Their cells fill with whatever new water they're in, equalizing the salinity between them but throwing all of their other chemical processes out of whack, killing them quickly.

This eel must have been just starting its journey south. I walked through the water behind it until it reached the rocks at the left end of the beach and disappeared into the darkness.

A minute after that, Noe and I did, too.

Bands of light from Bearskin Neck are filtering horizontally through the shallows in dull, diffuse shafts – the undersides of the reflections on the surface. Basketball-sized rocks break up the sand, and stands of tall, thin algae reach up to the surface bamboo-like in the darkness.

I haven't even adjusted my lights yet and a school of five squid is lined up across from us, hovering in the water like a squadron of tiny jet fighters. Each is whitish-gray and about three inches long, their arms pointed at us and the fins on the sides of their bodies undulating. Squid are everywhere in these waters during the summer and fall. It's hard to find them during the day, when they stay up in the water column and blend. At night, though, they're easy to spot against the black.

Noe and I swim toward them, not to get closer but to reach deeper water – we're not even in over our heads yet. The squid zip away into the darkness.
We work our way around the stands of tall algae and over an open sand flat. Crabs are scattered across it, many on their backs, grinding against the bottom. You wouldn't think their shells would get itchy but evidently they do. And they've been waiting all day for this. Crabs only flip over and expose their undersides in the dark when there are fewer predators about. I'm pretty sure turtle shells get itchy, too. When you dive in the Giant Ocean Tank at the New England Aquarium, Myrtle the Turtle practically accosts you to take a handful of sand and give her shell a scouring.

Another pair of squid, slightly larger, swims into

our lights and zips off. A third bops along an inch above the bottom, using the funnel on the underside of its body to shoot jets of water into the sand, looking for prey buried beneath. It stops, looks at us, then continues on.

We're still only ten feet deep. A squid more than a foot long, its body covered with iridescent blue spots, appears out of the darkness. It sees us and settles down on the bottom, arms resting on the sand in front of it. It's watching us and, as it does, I can almost feel its brain working. Like the octopus, squid are thinkers. Unlike octopus, they're social. I was once photographing a school of them lined up across from me in the water column. As I moved in closer and closer to the largest one, the rest closed ranks around me in a perfect circle, equidistant from one another, arms pointed toward me, watching and thinking whatever it is squid think.

Noe backs away from this one but I set down on the sand in front of it and move in closer, little by little, until I'm within three inches. It still doesn't move. I focus my camera on its large eye and squeeze off one shot. The strobes fire and the squid instantly springs up off the bottom and then, just as quickly, returns to the exact same spot.

I back away with Noe. The squid stays on the bottom, watching us. Thinking.

Another squid a foot in length appears out of the darkness, its body covered with reddish spots. It swims toward me, slowly, then changes direction and aims at Noe, swimming straight into his midsection, close enough that it's almost touching him. Noe backs up so he can see where the squid is (with a mask on, it's hard to see anything close to your chest) but it stays within inches of him.

Finally, it moves away and drops down a few inches off the sand, then comes in close to me. It isn't moving fast. It doesn't seem concerned. My hand is touching the sand and it backs up into my palm, touches it, then swims forward a few inches, reverses and swims back into my palm again. It stops to think about this, then rises straight up a foot and swims over my hand into open water. It's still in no hurry. As it swims, the red spots on its body fade to white and are replaced by a series of brown stripes. Like the octopus, its skin is filled with color-changing chromatophores. Most squid have about 30 different looks and can change to any of them in less than a second. And somehow, also like octopuses, they're almost certainly color blind.

Over the next 90 minutes, Noe and I meet up with another 40 or so squid. I have no idea where we are in relation to the beach but that's typical on a night dive. Wherever we are, we're 20 feet deep and I signal to him to surface so we can figure it out.

We head up and, as we do, we pass a small squid on the way. As I rise over it, it turns from white to deep red, drops its head, angles the back of its body sharply up toward the surface and throws all of its arms straight up, too. I'm now above it, rising, but I keep it in my lights as it repositions itself toward me and splays its arms wide. A second later, it drops two of its arms sharply down. Another second later, it bends down the tips of the arms that are still angled up. Call me crazy but this squid is trying to communicate. And it keeps trying until I'm too far above to see it anymore. The surface of the water is now just a few feet over me and I look straight up. Through it, stars shimmer in the night sky.

It was closing in on midnight by the time we stowed our gear. But the night was warm and beautiful and I was in no hurry to leave. Noe was with his wife, Martha, and their 14-year-old son, Gustavo, and they weren't in any hurry either. I cracked a cold beer (what the heck, it was late and no one was looking) and the four of us sat at the top of the seawall, looking out over the water.

A few minutes later, a pair of fishermen walked down and set themselves up at the water's edge. I knew they were fishing for stripers but we had just spent 90 minutes right where they were about to cast and we hadn't seen a single one. Noe and I looked at each other thinking the same thing – they were going to catch nothing.

In tandem, the two cast their lines out into the dark. Within seconds, both lines whipped taut, both rods bent and the dark water beyond started thrashing. They each reeled in a 10-pound striper.

Noe and I looked at each other again and laughed out loud. Every time you think you know what's down there, you find out you don't. Every time.

****

Three nights later, I made my way back to Gloucester well after dark and pulled into the lot at Folly

Cove. It was midweek and I assumed I'd have the place to myself. Seven cars were already there, though, and I had to squeeze into the last parking spot.

At Folly, there are no streetlights. And that night, there was no moon. The cove, the beach and the parking lot were all blanketed in dark. Country dark.

I stepped out of my car just as the guy parked beside me let out a string of what I assumed were Spanish expletives. He stood in his wetsuit staring into his trunk, his tank on the ground beside him rigged and ready to go. He slammed the trunk closed and started rooting through the back seat of his car. Only his feet stuck out through the open door. A guy parked on the other side of him, also rigged and ready to go, looked on forlornly. The first guy came up with a frustrated look and said something to his friend in Spanish.

"What did you forget?" I asked.

"My weight belt," he said, followed by some more possible expletives.

I have to take a step back here and say that of all the equipment divers wear, the weight belt may be the most mysterious to non-divers. Why need a weight belt when you already have a steel tank strapped onto your back?

The answer is simple: when you're trying to get underwater, it's not weight that's important but buoyancy. And scuba tanks, for all their weight, are hollow, filled with air and fairly buoyant. Some even float. It's the same principle that keeps steel ships on top of the water. There's no buoyancy in a lead weight, though. It just sinks – counteracting the buoyancy of a wetsuit and a tank and allowing divers to get underwater.

"Hold on a second," I said. "I might have some-thing." I've forgotten my fair share of gear over the years so when I see another diver in the same situation, I try to have his or her back. Daisy and Zeke sometimes left their weight belts in the car so I checked my trunk. There was a belt but it only had ten pounds on it.

"I usually wear 22," he said, then opened his trunk again to check for any loose leads. He had none. He said something in Spanish to his buddy but his buddy shook his head. He had no extras either.

"You should ask someone down there," I said, motioning toward divers I could hear talking down on the beach, invisible in the dark.

He padded off. His buddy looked at me and shook his head. I got the feeling this happened a lot.

Five minutes later, he came back. "Nope."

He and his buddy then had a conversation, the only part of which I understood was "*Adios.*" His buddy walked down the slope to dive by himself.

Twenty minutes later, the first guy backed out of the lot and drove off. And sometime after that, I walked down the slope, threaded my way through a group of wet divers and entered the water.

Hermit crabs of all sizes are sifting through the sand for food. Everywhere I point my lights, lobsters are walking – bumping into rocks, bumping into crabs, bumping into other lobsters. When they bump into each other, they jump up into the water column and land with their claws raised, ready to rumble.

Most of the lobsters are small. Many are missing a claw. Some are missing two. One hobbles over the sand missing both claws, three of its four legs on one side and two of the four on the other. If it survives long enough, they will all regenerate.

I reach the boulders on the right side of the cove and begin searching through the fronds of kelp blanketing them. A sculpin sleeps under one. A cunner sleeps under another. But the kelp is so thick that it's difficult to find anything.

In the darkness, a small face peers out from the thick, velvety stems of a clump of green fleece seaweed. With one finger, I ease the stems aside. It's a pipefish, a close relative of the seahorse. It actually looks like a seahorse that's been straightened out. It wriggles out and wraps around my finger. I raise it to my mask for a closer look, then move my hand back and jiggle my finger until it lets go and swishes back into the seaweed. As it does, something bumps into my leg and flips away. I don't even have to look to know it's a lobster.

When I dive here during the day, I spend most of my time over these boulders, or at the wall on the other side of the cove. At night, though, the sand is where things happen. I move out over it toward the middle of the cove, my lights illuminating the patches of sand in front of me as I pass one squadron of squid after another.

A lobster, larger than the others, walks out of the darkness and into my lights carrying a hermit crab tight in one claw. I have no idea why the lobster singled out this one poor hermit from the hundreds of others walking around. The lobster sees me and works its way cautiously around in a big arc, then continues off into the darkness.

A hake, six inches long, is swimming with a long pair of feelers on either side of its body sweeping the bottom, searching for prey under the sand.

Another swims by, paying me no attention. Suddenly it shudders and reverses direction to sweep back over the sand. It shudders again. Its body actually contorts a bit. It reverses direction, then dives head-first into the sand, disappearing underneath. A few seconds later it comes up on its side, just its head poking out. It sees me as if for the first time and slowly slides back into the sand until it's completely covered.

I keep moving over the sand until I reach the wall on the left side of the cove. A lone pollock – a foot long and greenish with a white lateral line along each side – is poking around in the rocks. During the day, pollock school up in the water column for protection. At night, though, they break apart to hunt. I have no idea how they find each other to re-form the school each morning. I move past it and it turns to swim with me, using my lights to help find prey.

Individual cod – almost identical to the pollock but reddish – are also poking about. Each is shier than the pollock and glides away when I get too close. Finally, one swims into my light and stays there. But its tail is gone – bitten clean off. It isn't bleeding and seems to be swimming without trouble. But it's hard to believe it can survive long down here without a tail fin.

I came out of the water two hours later onto the

dark beach, now empty, and was making my way up to the lot when someone called down to me.

"We've been watching your lights for almost an hour," he said with a Latino accent. "It was amazing. We could see everywhere you went. And whenever you took a photo, the flashes were like explosions!"

I reached the top of the slope and saw it was the buddy of the guy who had forgotten his weight belt. "Wow, you're still here," I said.

"Yeah, well, it's a beautiful night. You were going all over the cove. How did you know where you were?"

"I didn't," I said. "I was just following around behind whatever I was shooting."

"Let me give you a hand," he said. His wife stood beside him smiling. Over their shoulders in the dark, I could see two children sleeping in a mesh, fold-up tent with a small light inside. Theirs was the only other car still in the lot.

A tiny voice called from the tent.

"Hold on a second," he said, and started over to his kids. "Oh," he turned back, "your parking lights are on."

I looked over and saw them. "Oh, crap." Folly Cove was a bad place to be with a dead battery at midnight. It was isolated, unlit and cell phone coverage was spotty.

I rushed to take off my tank and get to my keys but the man's wife put a hand on my shoulder.

"Don't worry," she said, "my husband's a mechanic."

I finished taking off my gear, turned off my lights and turned on the ignition. It started up.

"Great," the man said from the tent.

A few minutes later, he called over while I was taking off my wetsuit. "We're going. Have a great night."

In the darkness, I hadn't realized they were packing up. His wife waved to me as they backed out and then they were gone.

That was a little weird, I thought. Why did they stay so long and then leave so fast? Then I remembered that he was a mechanic and realized they had waited in case my battery was dead and I needed a jump.

They knew, too, that Folly was a bad place to be with a dead battery at midnight, and they had my back.

****

My kayak bounced over the water, waves slapping its sides and reverberating against the hollow within. To starboard, the homes and storefronts of Bearskin Neck slipped by. Ahead, the Sandy Bay Breakwater – three hundred feet of massive granite blocks stacked on top of one another and rising 20 feet above the surface – grew closer and closer. My tank was rigged and strapped to the top of the forward hatch. My camera was strapped into the sternwell behind me. The rest of my gear was stowed below.

A mile offshore, I angled into the shadow of the breakwater. Dozens of seagulls and cormorants squatted on top of it, shrieking and cawing, raising their wings into the morning wind. I dropped anchor, made sure my tank, camera, and the rest of my gear were clipped in, then pushed them all overboard and rolled in myself to finish gearing up in the water.

    After the paddle out, the cool water feels great. I'm dropping down the anchor line, paying out at a 45-degree angle. A group of hake, about ten of them, all about a foot long, is lying on the sand in a herring-bone pattern.

    I'm 40 feet from the breakwater but can see its blocks clearly. As neatly as they're stacked above water, here they angle down to the sand in a chaotic jumble.

    Smaller details come into focus as I swim closer – cuts on the blocks' edges and broken corners, the beds of blue mussels covering parts of them, and sea stars scattered over their faces. Moon jellies pulse along up near the surface. From almost every crevice, a lobster looks out at me. Fish are everywhere. Most are cunner, swimming about the blocks. Sculpin and sea raven are lying on flat ledges. I straddle the edge of one block and stare up into the glare of the sun. Hundreds of fish are silhouetted against it.

    I push away and angle back down toward the sand, passing crabs scurrying around small sea peaches and groups of frilled anemones. A lone dogfish glides by. I used to see great schools of these small sharks. No more, though. I wonder what it's like to be programmed to spend your life in a group but to have no group to spend it with.

    I'm almost to the bottom when a torpedo ray, its body a thick, dark disk three feet in diameter, lifts up from the sand and swims just over it. Unlike most rays that flap the sides of their bodies like wings, the torpedo ray swings its heavy tail from side to side. Thirty feet from where it took off, it settles back down, then rises up and sets down again, covering itself with a thin layer of sand.

I stop and kneel down a few feet in front of it. It stares back at me, unafraid. Torpedo rays have electric organs just under their skin that can deliver more than 200 volts – enough to knock you unconscious.

I'd love to see this one up in the water again, swimming. I kick back up the side of the breakwater and take a seat on the end of a block, giving the torpedo space. A minute later, it lifts up and sets back down forcefully, completely covering itself with sand. It's not going anywhere.

I don't mind. I've got a great spot and plenty of air. I lean back against the block, taking in as much of it as I can.

****

"So, this dive is *just* to catch lobsters?" Zeke asked as we looked out over the flat water.

"Yes."

"And nothing else?"

"Yes," I said again. "Wait ... what are you talking about?"

"You're not bringing your camera?"

"No, I'm not bringing my camera." I actually was going to but not now. The camera would stay in the car.

Zeke nodded, satisfied.

He had just gotten his first lobster license, allowing him to hand-catch up to 15 lobsters a day from a half hour after sunrise to a half hour before sunset anywhere in Massachusetts. It was the next phase of my plan to keep him interested in diving. The problem was that we should have done this back in July, not in September, after hundreds of other divers had been combing the bottom catching them.

We're heading out over the sand straight to the boulders and ledges at the right end of the beach. The water is warm and clear and visibility is 20 feet. Almost immediately, Zeke spots a lobster on the sand, skirting the edge of the rocks. It's a little guy that weighs about a pound. Zeke looks at him, then at me. It's too small and he knows it. I motion for him to grab it – better to practice on small ones than big ones.

The lobster faces us and raises its claws. Zeke angles over it, then reaches in quickly and grabs it by the shell just behind its head. The lobster arches back as far as it can, stretching its claws out wide.

Zeke fumbles with the gauge (you have to measure the length of the lobster's carapace to determine if it's legal), trying to operate it with one hand while holding onto the lobster with the other. After a few failed attempts, he holds the lobster out to me. He has to learn to do this by himself but it's his first time so I reach out to help. The lobster quickly grabs my thumb and pinches. *Yeoww!* I'm wearing quarter-inch neoprene gloves and the lobster only weighs a pound but it can pinch. I shake its claw loose from my hand, take hold of it by the shell and hand it back to Zeke when he's ready. He measures it, confirms that it's well short of legal and sets it down on the sand. It scoots backward into the rocks.

We continue out. There are quite a few lobsters walking about and Zeke catches them one after another but every one is undersized. He catches two that are very close. Both times, he holds them up to me with the gauge to their shells and both times they're legal by a hair. My instinct is to let them go but I want him to have a successful dive and bring home dinner, so I give him the 'okay' sign. Both times he shakes his head and sets them down to scoot away.

Finally, 40 minutes in, he sees a three-pounder tucked in deep under a boulder. He presses himself down to the sand and reaches in but the lobster's too far back. Zeke repositions himself to reach in farther. Still no. Two tries later, he looks at me and shakes his head. Then he wraps his arms around himself. He's either signaling that he's cold or that he needs a hug. I assume it's cold and we start in.

Along the way, I look under every rock and boulder we pass, really wanting him to catch a good-sized lobster, but we don't see another one.

We surfaced exactly an hour after we went in.

"Sorry you didn't get any," I said. "It's late in the year to be catching them from the beach. We'll start earlier next year."

"That's all right," Zeke said. "I think it was one of

my best dives."

"Really?"

"Yeah, it was great."

"Why?"

He shrugged. "I had a good time."

I nodded, taking it as a small victory.

Fall

Ten hours after leaving my house, after driving through Franconia Notch in New Hampshire and the Northeast Kingdom in Vermont, after crossing the border into Canada, driving through Quebec City and sharing a ferry with a convoy of tractor trailer trucks crossing the Saguenay River, I pulled into the parking lot of the Essipit First Nation Reserve in Escoumins, Quebec. Ed and Edna would be arriving shortly on a different ferry.

"*Bonjour!*" a young woman in the office said when I walked in.

"*Bonjour,*" I said. "*Parlez-vous anglais?*"

The woman half smiled, half grimaced, then said something so fast I wasn't sure what language she had said it in. I was pretty sure it wasn't English, though. I handed her a printout of the email confirmation they had sent me earlier. I had stayed on the reserve before, in a complex of condos they rent out on the banks of the St. Lawrence. This time, though, I had waited too long to make a reservation and there were no condos left. But they seemed to have something for us. I just wasn't sure what.

"*Ah,*" she said, brightening. She took the paper and, with a big smile, pointed back up the road as she explained something in French.

"*Je suis désolé mais je ne parle pas français,*" I said, using one of my memorized phrases. I'm sorry but I don't speak French.

She grimaced again, sympathetically, then glanced around at her co-workers. Clearly, neither of them spoke English either. She picked up a map and held it out to me.

"*Lac Jeemy,*" she said very slowly, enunciating.

"*Lac Jeemy?*"

"*Oui, Lac Jeemy.*"

I had to laugh. "Okay, *Lac Jeemy*. I have no idea what that means."

The woman laughed, too. "*Jeemy,*" she said several more times, hoping the repetition would help. It didn't. She closed her eyes, still smiling but trying to transition from the routine of her day to the challenge of communicating with a non-French speaker.

"Like *Endreex,*" she finally said

That sounded familiar. "*Endreex?*" I said. "You mean, Hendrix?"

She nodded happily.

I had my air guitar right there and I pulled it out and played the opening chords of *Purple Haze*. "Jimi Hendrix?"

"*Oui!*" she said, "*Jeemy Endreex!*"

Ah, and '*lac*' ... lake?

"*Oui!*"

Now, we were getting somewhere. Or not. I still didn't have clue about where Ed, Edna, and I would be sleeping.

But after a few more minutes of pointing at the

map, drawing lines and circles on it, and gesturing toward the road and the clock, I started to understand. We wouldn't be staying on the reserve. We would be staying at Lake Jimmy, which was about 20 minutes down the road and marked by a set of large teepee poles.

After many '*merci beaucoups*,' I walked out of the office and into my car. She had told me to turn right out of the parking lot but I still had to meet Ed and Edna at the ferry, so I drove out and turned left. I had no doubt she was watching and shaking her head.

I pulled up to the crowded landing just as cars were starting to roll off the ferry. The Diver Ed Mobile was among the first. People all over the dock stopped and turned to stare at the gaudy truck. Expressions ran the gamut from amused to confused to amazed. Then dozens of cell phones rose up in the air. People were photographing Ed and Edna as they drove up the ramp.

Sure enough, 20 minutes later, we pulled off the road at a set of large teepee poles. Inside a log cabin office, two men, one in his twenties, the other in his fifties, stood behind the counter. "*Bonjour!*" the young man said.

"*Bonjour*," I said. "*Parlez-vous anglais?*"

Both men smiled but shook their heads.

I handed the young man the reservation printout. He busied himself with it then looked at us again. "So ... no French at all?" he asked in halting English.

"*Non*," I said.

"What are you talking about," Ed cut in. "I speak French." He spread his arms and legs wide and began to sing *Lady Marmalade*, his hips thrusting suggestively.

Voulez-vous coucher avec moi,
ce soir?

This caught me by surprise. I was even more surprised when I began to sing with him. Not *Lady Marmalade* but the French bits from the Beatles' *Michelle*, with my face set in the most sincere Paul McCartney-like expression I could manage.

Michelle, ma belle,
Sont les mots qui vont très bien ensemble,
très bien ensemble,

The two men stared at us, then burst out laughing. And clapping.

"*Très bonne!*" the young man yelled, reaching across the counter to slap me on the shoulder.

A few hand gestures and some broken English later, I understood that we were to get back in our cars and follow the older man to our chalet. As we pulled out, the young man emerged from the office with a shotgun on his shoulder. He gave a quick wave and marched off.

We started down a rocky, dirt road into a dense forest, winding up and down and around. A mile and a half in, we passed a broken-down car pushed off to the side of the road and wrapped up like a Christmas present in police CAUTION tape.

Another half-mile in, the road forked and we

followed a sign pointing to the *Geai Bleu Chalet*. I started wondering what kind of impression we had made in the office. And then we were there.

The *Geai Bleu* turned out to be more rustic than it sounded. The chalet was a cabin with two bedrooms, each of which had five bunks. There was electricity but no electrical outlets. There was running water but it wasn't safe to drink. There was a bathroom but it was basically an indoor outhouse. And the refrigerator didn't work.

We couldn't have been happier. The *Geai Bleu* faced out over the now-famous *Lac Jimmy*, across the surface of which a huge beaver was casually swimming on its back, meandering this way and that. We settled in, built a fire and ate dinner under the stars at a picnic table overlooking the water.

All along the main road in downtown Escoumins, streetlights are decorated with long, vertical banners of crabs and nudibranchs and anemones. There are streets named after marine animals. There's at least one restaurant with photos of ocean pout and wolffish and hermit crabs varnished into the table tops. Nowhere in the world have I met people more proud of the marine life that surrounds them.

They even have a marine park set up specifically for divers. Ed's truck was already parked outside its locked gate the next morning when I pulled in behind him. The park was closed for the season, with no access to its office, locker rooms, bathrooms or showers. But I walked around the gate and in. A handful of the park's employees were still about and the part of me

Ed gearing up on the stage platform at the marine park. From here, you cross over the rocks and then down into the St. Lawrence. Photo: Edna Martin

that's become used to 'No Trespassing' signs and liability waivers half expected them to yell at me in French to get out.

"*Bonjour!*" they called.

Down on the rocks, a wooden, stage-like platform overlooked the water. Ed was already putting his gear together and Edna was sitting in the sun, reading. A pod of minke whales cruised by on the surface, a stone's throw from the rocks. A pod of belugas passed by just after that. I walked back to my car and carried my gear down.

The water is 38 degrees with sunlight streaming down onto boulders covered with polar sea stars – they look like common sea stars but are more green. The sea stars quickly disappear as the bottom slopes sharply away.

The ledge that starts above on the surface drops down the slope like a giant staircase covered with knobby anemones, frilled anemones and northern red anemones. Sponges are everywhere. So are sea cucumbers and scarlet psoluses – much like the sea cucumbers but brilliantly red. Scattered in between them are the largest sunstars I've ever seen – fat and purple and close to two feet across. As at Deer Island Point, there's so much that it's hard to focus in on any one thing. And the problem is magnified by great visibility. I can see 50 feet in every direction.

All along the ledge, snow crabs – long-legged and spidery – stare out from under the tentacles of northern reds, using them for protection. A small jelly pulses by, its innards impossibly white within its bell.

Forty feet below the surface, the ledge ends. Boulders are scattered down the slope beyond it. Like the ledge, all are covered with invertebrates. A large cod – two feet long and heavy-bodied – sees me and swims under one of them.

I follow the boulders vertically down the slope. A wolffish – brown instead of blue like those farther south – stares out from under one, its eyes rolling this way and that as if on gimbals.

I check my computer and can't believe I'm 140 feet deep. It's not the depth that surprises me but how quickly I reached it. I thought I was half that. I kick back up the slope. As I do, small shannies splotched red and white wriggle away eel-like to hide under rocks. Rosefish hang in the water just above the bottom, watching.

I make it back to the ledge and see one northern red that looks different – its tentacles somehow longer than they should be. I kick in closer. They aren't tentacles at all but the long legs of a snow crab, splayed out sideways as its body is pulled into the anemone's mouth, fraction of an inch by fraction of an inch, for long minutes until the last bit of it disappears and the anemone closes up over it. Hiding under them for protection is a dangerous game.

I kick back across the ledge to a nylon line anchored three feet above the bottom. It's covered with hydroids and nudibranchs and leads straight up the slope to the steps – a marker for divers.

I'm not ready to surface yet, though. I rise 30 feet up into the water column and float there face-down, taking a bird's-eye view of the life and color and movement everywhere around the boulders below.

The next morning, we left *Geai Bleu* and drove back along the St. Lawrence, winding through more pine forests, around massive rock cliffs and beside whitewater rapids, all the way to the Saguenay River. We pulled in to Sainte Rose du Nord, a cul-de-sac that seems to have been lifted straight up from the French Alps and dropped down here.

The sounds of French bubbled up all around us. A ferry was coming into the quay and people waiting for it milled about. As always, Ed's truck attracted attention and a steady flow of Quebecers, whose English ranged from the equivalent of our French to almost fluent, came

The quay reaching out into the Saguenay. We made our first dive on this side of it, moving parallel to the shore. We made our second dive on the opposite side of it.

in for a closer look. None seemed surprised to see divers. An elderly woman sidled up to me. "The marine life," she said, "it is beautiful, *oui*?"

Even though the water temperature was in the 30s, on land it was close to 90 degrees – a warm day for late September in Quebec. With sweat streaming down my face, I pulled on my heavy thermals, zipped into my drysuit and emptied a jug of water over my head to cool off. Ed was bent over beside his truck, adjusting his weight belt and singing to himself – something about a wonderful time with Jerry Shine. But it was too hot to stop and listen. I hustled along a path that led to the left of the quay, then down the rocks and into the water.

Ed looks like something from a low-budget horror movie made in the 1960s. He's sepia. And kind of fuzzy.

The top 30 feet of the Saguenay River is fresh water and heavily tannic from decomposing plant life, giving everything – the rubble bottom, the fallen branches scattered over it, Ed – a gauzy, brownish-yellow look.

We're following the slope down and away from the pier and reach the halocline – the interface between the fresh water on top and the salt water below – and pass through it. It's like swimming through salad dressing. For a few moments, everything looks oily and out of focus.

And then we're through, into pitch black. We're 35 feet deep on a sunny day but absolutely no light is filtering through the tannic water above. None. We're in the blackest black I've ever seen.

As black as the water is, it's also crystal clear and visibility is incredible. Ed is moving fast and is 40 feet ahead of me but I can see him clearly in the glow of his lights. He's aiming his lights another 30 feet or so ahead and I can see the bottom along the entire length of their beam. Visibility is at least 100 feet.

I adjust one of my strobes and the motion sends muck from the bottom swirling up into the water column. It's kind of beautiful how it dances in the light but I pump a blast of air into my BC and rise a few feet to keep from kicking up any more.

Other than the brown of the muck, there's almost no color here. But we're moving deeper and the bottom abruptly changes to a sheer rock face – just like the cliffs

we drove through to get here – with small ledges breaking out here and there. I settle down on one, switch off
my lights and sit for a few moments in the blackness. It's
hard to believe the rest of the world is just 100 feet above.
It feels much farther away than that.

Ed's lights are glowing ahead. I switch mine back
on. On top of the muck gathered in a rocky corner in
front of me, a trio of northern cerianthids, with long,
slender tentacles, purple and white, is swaying in the water. There's another quartet of them a few feet away on
another patch of muck. The more I look, the more I see.
Groups of them are all over the ledge, everywhere muck
has gathered.

I lift up as motionlessly as possible and set down
on another ledge farther down the wall. A shrimp with
huge, ball-shaped eyes and a translucent body with red
stripes and blue spots, clings to the vertical rock face,
arching back enough to look straight at me. Three more
cling to different levels of the ledge alongside it. Peering
out from a crevice, a juvenile ocean pout, its head the size
of a golf ball, watches me. I move in and its big pectorals
fan slightly, moving it back deeper into the crevice. I back
away and it comes forward an equal amount. I move in, it
pulls back.

I take a quick look at my computer. The water is
36 degrees and I'm 118 feet deep. This is deeper than I
want to be – I want to conserve air and stay under as long
as possible – so I rise 30 feet up the wall. As I do, I pass a
dozen rosefish, all moving slowly with their bellies to the
wall, treating it as if it's the bottom.

I pull alongside Ed and set down on another
ledge. Cerianthids cover it. So do shrimp – some like the

ones I saw earlier but others longer and sleeker, red with a yellow oval on the tops of their heads.

Ed has pulled ahead of me again and gone deeper. He's hanging in the black water in front of a sheer rock face, his lights glowing in the darkness. As I watch him, something looks familiar. It takes a few seconds but then I realize – he looks like one of the last scenes in *The Abyss*, when Ed Harris is dropping down a rock face through the blackness holding an underwater flare. If only I had a wide-angle lens – I would love a shot of this.

I take a look at my air. It's time to start back. Ed waves his lights. He's heading back, too. I try to use every second I have left to see everything I can – the colonies of cerianthids, the rosefish, the shrimp. I leave the navigation to Ed, paying no attention to where we are. When he heads up, I head up with him, through the oily halocline into the tannic fresh water and up the sepia slope. After the salt water, the fresh water feels wonderfully soft. I take my time and eventually stop, letting Ed's fins kick up and away in the brownish-yellow gauze.

After an hour on the surface, sweating in the noon heat, Ed and I walked down a boat ramp on the right side of the quay. The wind had picked up and two- to three-foot whitecaps were pounding the shore. The sweat in my eyes was making it hard to see but I walked into the tannic water and the relief from the heat was instant.

We've just gone under and a lion's mane jelly

is pulsing in front of me. The whitish-blue of its bell against the tannic water looks very cool and I try to line it up for a shot. But I'm still shallow enough that the waves overhead are pulling me up and down. And in the tannic light, the camera's autofocus is ratcheting back and forth, trying to lock onto something without any luck.

Ed's only five feet away but in the low viz, he seems very distant. I turn back to the lion's mane and move in as close as possible. At last, I squeeze off one shot.

I turn back to Ed but he's gone.

I start down the slope, too. It's much more gradual on this side of the quay but the current is pushing hard from behind and, in seconds, I've zoomed through the halocline into salt water. Instead of following a course away from the quay as we did on the first dive, we're staying alongside it here, following it straight out. All around me, bright shrimp and big yellow nudibranchs zoom past, standing out against the brown muck.

I think I see the glow of Ed's lights up ahead but I'm not sure. Visibility is terrible – even here in the salt water. It's still pitch black, though.

There's no rock ledge but there is a lot of junk – old tires, barrels, twisted pieces of metal. Much of it is unidentifiable. Tree trunks and big branches are mixed in, too. I turn to a colorful shrimp tucked in beside a yellow anemone and try to concentrate on it but the current is pushing me away from the shore, even though I'm facing into it, kicking and trying to hold my position. I look around for Ed's lights but still don't see them.

The strength of the current has caught me by surprise. I haven't dived here much but I've never had to deal with current here before. I fight my way back up the slope to a bright orange anemone. Beside it, a beautiful shrimp with the largest eyes I've ever seen stares at me from the top of a rock. I move in close to photograph it but suddenly the current picks up even more. Silt washes down over the rock and the water looks greasy. The current is so strong that it's pushing fresh water all the way down here, 90 feet below the surface.

I reach out to grab the rock but the current slides under me and lifts me off the bottom. Suddenly I'm being swept down the slope fast until I find a rock to grab onto.

This is not good. I take another look around for Ed's lights, then pull myself up on the rock. Ahead, I see nothing else to grab. I press myself to the muck, kicking it up all around me, and dig into the bottom with my knees and fins and start crawling, making slow headway against the current.

After five minutes, and having left a trench behind me, I pass through the halocline into fresh water and the current dies off. I swim along the bottom into the shallows, then pop up in waist-deep water.

Moments later, Ed popped up a few feet away, his face barely breaking the surface. There were no "Woohoos!" There was no tremendous laughter.

We stared at each other in a strange silence for a few moments.

"That current sucked," I finally said.

"I know!" Ed said, re-animating.

Edna walked down the boat ramp toward us. The

wind had died down and in the short time we were under, the waves had all but flattened.

"You guys really stuck together," Edna said when she reached us.

I looked at Ed in surprise, then back at her. "We weren't together at all."

"Yeah, I took off when I saw you shooting that jelly!" Ed laughed/yelled. "I couldn't believe you were shooting that. I thought, I'm not waiting here while Jerry Shine shoots a jelly!"

"Well, I watched your bubbles the whole time," Edna said, "you guys were never more than 20 feet apart."

Daylight was fading fast as I drove back to *Geai Bleu*, a cloud of dust rising up on the dirt road behind me. It was our last night in Quebec and Ed and Edna were in town picking up groceries.

As I pulled up to the chalet, my car suddenly let out a high-pitched grinding noise that sent a chill down my back. It sounded like a power saw trying to cut through a cinder block. Car trouble two miles up a dirt road in the woods, in a place where almost no one spoke English, the night before I was supposed to leave, was not what I wanted.

I parked the car and popped the hood, hoping to see a branch stuck in the fan belt or something dragging underneath – some easy fix. But I saw nothing. Every worst-case scenario began running through my mind. I was going to have to get towed out of the woods. I was going to have to find a mechanic. I was going to have to get around somehow while he worked on it. And I was going to have to do it all without being able to speak French.

A few minutes later, Ed and Edna pulled in. Ed looked at my hood propped open. "Please tell me you just decided to check your oil."

"I wish," I said. "Something's grinding in there."

Ed sighed. "Start it up for me."

I did and it sounded fine – until I put it in gear and drove forward a few feet. Then the quiet of the woods was destroyed. The grinding carried out over Lac Jimmy and echoed through the forest.

A worried look flashed over Ed's face. "That's not good." He stared at the engine, now rumbling quietly. "Put it in reverse."

I did and the grinding rose up again until he held up his hand.

"Now come forward."

I grinded toward him.

Back and forth we went, and each time, Ed moved a little closer to the driver's side, listening. At last, he was on the ground beside the left front tire.

"I bet there's a rock in there bouncing around."

He grabbed the jack out of my trunk, pushed me out of the way and jacked the car up. He pulled the tire off and rooted around behind the wheel hub. "Here it is!" he yelled. A second later, he stood up with a big smile on his face, holding out the offending stone.

And just like that, all of my worst-case scenarios disappeared. I looked at Ed – at smiling, beautiful Diver Ed – and felt a love for him like I had never felt for a man before. "Come here, you," I said, pulling him in with a big bear hug.

We put the tire back on and were just taking

the car down off the jack when Daisy called. I told her the story, complete with imitations of the grinding and descriptions of the cold sweat running down my back, feeling like a death row inmate who had just received a last-minute pardon.

"Well, you can go anywhere in the world you want," Daisy finally said, "but you have to take Ed with you."

That was fine with me.

Later, I made a pasta dinner for the three of us. As it cooked, we sat at the picnic table – relaxed, beers in hand, looking out over the lake. The beaver appeared on the surface again but this time it was booking, swimming fast.

"Man, look at the wake he's leaving," Ed said, pointing at the long V trailing behind it. "He's like the Loch Ness Monster – he's the Lac Jimmy Monster!"

We ate under the stars and never did a pasta dinner with bottled sauce taste so good.

****

Dolibers Cove in Marblehead, Massachusetts is a picturesque little place – a tiny beach lined with multi-million dollar homes. I pulled in under a blue sky dotted with the whitest of clouds. Overhead, a flock of starling spiraled acrobatically, flowing over a few lone but massive trees. The yard of the house across the road was decked out with silver, life-sized aliens – Halloween decorations. A few minutes later, Andy Martinez pulled in and parked behind me.

Andy, a retired schoolteacher, authored *Marine Life of the North Atlantic*, the bible of marine life identification in the northeast. He was also a Jim Croce *doppelgänger* and the only person I knew who actually went to Woodstock (leading to frequent jokes about his having ignored the warnings to stay away from the brown acid). I couldn't believe it was October and this was our first dive of the year together.

We walked down to the little beach. There were no waves but a surge moved through the water palpably before hitting the shore. It wasn't bad enough to call the dive. But it was bad enough that visibility was going to be terrible.

"You want to try somewhere else?" I asked.

Andy stared at the water. I could tell he wanted to dive here. I did, too. From the surface, the little cove looked like any other but, for reasons unknown, it attracts invasive species rarely seen anywhere else in the area. And it does so in incredible numbers.

"Let's give it a shot," Andy said, setting his huge camera down at the water's edge.

We've been underwater for less than a minute and the sunshine, the blue skies and the puffy clouds are all distant memories. It's murky. And green. Visibility is less than three feet and I've already lost track of Andy.

The bottom is a mix of cobble and sand with a few rock ledges pushing up. Minute after minute passes

Dolibers Cove, for reasons unkown, attracts incredible numbers of invasive shrimp and crabs.

and I don't see anything. A flash of light cuts through the murk. Then another. Then a whole bunch. Andy's photographing something. I'm tempted to swim over but force myself not to. There's plenty to see and shoot, I just need to slow down and look for it.

I settle down on the cobble and lean in close to a group of softball-sized rocks. It takes a few seconds but a shrimp seems to materialize on top of one. It's about an inch long and translucent, its body lined with burgundy stripes, its legs with yellow bars. It's a European rock shrimp, an invasive species I've only seen here.

As I look, three more appear on the rocks around it. I start to move over the bottom and soon they're everywhere within my limited viz.

I reach the sand at the end of the cobble, and small crabs – some white, some white and green, some green and orange – are scurrying sideways all over it.

They're juvenile green crabs. They're also invasive but have been here so long and become so common that it's hard to think of them as invasive. I've never seen them colored like this, though.

I move back over the cobble and lift the end of a rock that's about two feet long. Four crabs, all about an inch from side to side, with heavy claws and yellowish bodies covered with burgundy spots stare up at me, stunned at their sudden exposure. They scatter sideways in four different directions. Within seconds, they're all re-hidden. They're Asian shore crabs and, like the European rock shrimp, I've never seen them anywhere else but here.

I lift another rock. There are three more. Two scurry away after the shock of being outed. The third, the largest, stares up at me, refusing to move. The crab takes a tentative step sideways but stops and waits until I lower the rock back down. I move on across the bottom and every rock I lift has three to six of them hiding underneath.

Forty minutes later, with plenty of air left, I decide to head in. The viz is just too bad. I start back over the cobble but stop in front of a shrimp that has something in its claws. The shrimp is less than an inch in length and whatever it's holding is only a fraction of that. I swing a magnifier over my camera port and take another look. The shrimp is holding a tiny crab – a crab about one-quarter the size of a pencil eraser. The crab is a local species and it's staring straight up at the shrimp – the two of them face-to-face. I'm looking over the top of the crab's shell, seeing the shrimp as the crab must see it, and the shift in perspective is jarring. Suddenly, the shrimp doesn't look so harmless. Right now it looks huge and merciless. I'm glad I'm not the crab.

****

"We have you in a Chevy Spark," the rental agent said. "Perhaps I could put you into something a little bigger."

"The Spark will be fine," I said, having no idea just how small the Spark really was. I needed to get from the airport to the Blue Heron Bridge as quickly as possible and didn't have time to sort through other cars. Ed and Edna had driven all the way down from Maine and were already there. So far, my plane had landed on time, my bags had come out quickly and I was the first in line here. If everything kept falling my way, I'd be able get to the bridge in time to dive with them on the tide.

"The Bruins are heating up," the agent said without looking up from his keyboard. Once again, my hat. "They just did a number on the two Florida teams."

"Don't hold it against me."

"Oh, I'm not a fan of either Florida team," he said, still tapping away. I detected a trace of a Canadian accent but didn't have time to engage.

Twenty minutes later, I zipped the Spark (it really was very small) into the Blue Heron Bridge parking lot and pulled in beside Ed.

"Woo-hoo!" he yelled, pulling gear from the back of a gray pick-up truck.

"Where's the Diver Ed mobile?"

"We had to get rid of it," he yelled. "The whole

underside was rusted out from salt water. We're lucky it didn't fall off in the middle of the road."

I looked at the new truck skeptically. It certainly lacked the personality of the Diver Ed Mobile. But the importance of an intact underside couldn't be overstated.

It was a beautiful November day, but well over 90 degrees. I hadn't expected it to be so hot. Or so crowded.

"I don't think I've ever seen so many divers in one place," Edna said, setting up her tank. Divers were gearing up all across the parking lot and the beach. None that I knew, though. Ariane was in New York, Anne had packed up her gear for the season and Sandra had jury duty. Ed and Edna had never dived here before, though, and I couldn't wait for them to see it.

The water is 82 degrees. I've been under for less than 30 seconds and half a dozen moon jellies – their aqua bells a foot across – are pulsing just under the surface. One bumps my hand and feels like a piece of hard plastic.

We swim out and away from the bridge heading right. Large cushion stars – heavy-bodied, brownish-yellow sea stars a foot across – are scattered over the bottom, all moving, all sifting through the sand in slow-motion, hard-target searches for buried shellfish. An upside-down jelly pulses on the bottom, its tentacles amber and green. There are no nudibranchs eating it from within. Or none large enough that I can see. I keep moving over the sand, over a dozen hermit crabs, all of whom tuck into their shells as I pass.

Out of the corner of my eye, I see a flying gurnard moving across the bottom. Its wing-like pectoral fins are pulled into its body but it's dragging its pelvic fins – lower on its body – along the sand, chemically searching for prey. The gurnard stops, tips to one side and three short rays at the base of that pectoral separate out and tap the bottom. Then it rights itself and moves on.

Over and over, it does this, but every time, it rights itself and keeps swimming. I get too close and it fans open its pectorals fully like the dinosaur that eats Newman in *Jurassic Park*. I back off and it pulls its fins in and continues over the sand.

I have no idea where Ed or Edna are. I move back in toward the stanchions of the bridge. Scrums of fireworms are everywhere, tangled up like balls of white and orange yarn. I pass over the disembodied head of a fish, probably thrown in by a fisherman after being cleaned, and fireworms are crawling all over it. In other places, they cover urchins.

Something slashes in front of me, roiling the bottom. The sand settles and a sand diver – a fish about a foot long and looking like a large penis – stares at me before slashing away.

Farther on, six white strands stretch out 18 inches from a tiny hole in the rubble like so many pasta vectors. It's a spaghetti worm, its body hidden in a tube underground while its arms hunt for dead plankton above. A few feet away, an octopus rises up from a hole in the sand then retracts when I get close.

The inside of my mouth feels incredibly dry and

both of my calves are starting to cramp. I'm dehydrated from the flight, the sudden Florida heat and the breathing of dry tank air for three hours. I grab the tip of one fin and pull it toward me to stretch out my calf, then switch and pull the other fin. This usually works but these cramps are refusing to de-cramp. I'm now at the point where every kick, even little ones, sends my calf muscles into painful knots. Finally, I stop kicking altogether and swim with just my arms, breaststroke style.

As always, the bridge supports are teeming with angelfish, some yellow and black, others yellow and blue. There are big green parrotfish, puffers, barracuda and dozens of other tropical fish I can't identify. All around the supports, trios and quartets and more of spiny lobsters stare out from under ledges and rocks, their antennae waving and so intertwined that it's impossible to tell whose are whose. Unlike northern lobsters, they have no claws – which is one of the reasons they aren't really lobsters. The two aren't even closely related.

I move back out over the sand as a huge eagle ray glides straight toward me, about five feet off the bottom. It rises up until it's just under the surface and passes straight overhead, flapping the sides of its body like wings, while its long tail trails behind.

I hobbled back up onto the beach stiff-legged, both of my calves almost too cramped to walk. Ed was already there. "Oh, my God," he yelled, eyes wide. "That was unbelievable! I – why are you walking like that?"

An hour later, we sat in an indoor/outdoor tiki restaurant a mile from the water. Ed's voice was still lodged up in a higher register, talking about shrimp and blennies and batfish and crabs. Edna was thrilled, too, talking along just under him, adding details here and there, providing exclamation and bringing up creatures Ed had forgotten.

"And did you see that penis fish?" Ed asked Edna. He must have meant the sand diver. "Oh, my God, he was on the sand in front of me and I just couldn't stop looking at him. I mean I just couldn't stop. I want to have my penis tattooed to look just like him, with the same color patterns and the eyes and the teeth and the gills ... everything!"

Edna didn't seem averse to the idea.

Ed turned back to me. "So what's next after you finally finish this book?" he asked, his voice dropping back into a lower register.

"I'm just focused on this one."

"Yeah, but you must have something in mind," he pressed. (It sounds self-serving but this conversation really did happen.)

"Well, I've been thinking about chartering a boat and cruising down what's left of the Intercoastal with Daisy and Zeke. But it's all so preliminary that I wouldn't even call it preliminary."

"That would be great," Ed said, his voice moving back up into the higher register. "If you did it in the fall, you could take the *Starfish Enterprise*."

I stared at Ed in disbelief. That boat was his livelihood and here he was offering it to me for a 6,000-mile round-trip voyage. "I couldn't do that unless you guys came," I said.

"No, we have other things to do in the fall," Ed

said. "But the boat doesn't have any living quarters so you'd have to rent a trailer and put it on the back deck."

I took a sip of beer, wondering what Edna was thinking about this. The *Starfish Enterprise* was her livelihood, too.

"Actually," she said, "you'll need two trailers since Zeke will want to have his own space. He's not going to want to live in the same trailer as his parents."

"Yeah, that will be so cool," Ed said. "It will be like his own little apartment!"

I took another sip of beer while Ed and Edna planned out the logistics of the trip and the changes they were going to have to make to the boat to accommodate it. There was no way I was going to take the *Starfish Enterprise*. But once again, as I listened to them, I could feel my heart filling with love for these two people.

When I pulled in the next morning, Ed was talking to a diver I didn't know. I got out of the Spark and walked over to them stiff-legged, elbows jerking up with each step, my calves still painful from yesterday's dive.

"Man, you walk like Walter Brennan," Ed said.

"Yeah, now I know why he walked that way." I leaned against a picnic table and pushed on it, trying to stretch out my calf muscles.

The other diver introduced himself as Markus. "You should eat a banana," he said, holding one out to me.

I've spent most of my life declining such offers and was about to do so again. But the thought of how badly cramped I'd be after another long dive today changed my mind.

"Thanks," I said, taking it and wolfing it down.

He handed me another. "I have a whole bunch."

It turned out that Markus had moved to Florida specifically for the diving and had spent so much time underwater here that he could pinpoint the locations for quite a bit of life. I told him we'd be heading to the smaller bridge at the left end of the beach.

"When you start to bend around toward the bridge, there are a pair of jawfish side-by-side in the sand," he said. "And there are a lot hermit crabs, too, big ones. And after you pass the first and second sunken boats, look inside the third – it's full of spiny lobsters."

At the next table down, I saw Connie Bishop – Joe George's wife – and her friend Claire LeBlanc gearing up. Joe hadn't been able to come down but Connie and Claire were here for a dive show later in the week. I didn't know Claire well but she and Connie were two of the quietest people I had ever met. Especially when they were talking.

"Where are you guys heading?" I asked.

"Oh, probably out that way," Connie said with a softly clipped Canadian accent, pointing to the right. "Or maybe that way," she said, pointing straight out. Then her voice dropped. "Where do you want to go?" she asked Claire, not whispering but her voice somehow quieter than any whisper I had ever heard.

"Well, we could head that way ..." Claire said. I leaned in as her voice trailed off. It was still audible to Connie, somehow, who responded even more quietly. For the next minute or so, I watched their lips moving, and heard faint murmurs coming from their mouths, but nothing loud enough for me to understand.

The small bridge at Blue Heron. The larger bridge is behind me.

Connie finally turned back to me. "We don't really know," she laughed. Softly.

"All right. Well, we're heading that way," I said, pointing to the left. "So maybe we'll see you down there."

As the incoming tide fell slack, Ed, Edna and I walked across the beach and into the water. Ed was behind me, singing, of course.

> *I met a handsome diver*
> *and his name was Jerry Shine*

Immediately, my senses jolted to high alert. Ed's pre-dive ditties were usually crooning ballads. But this one was upbeat. It was peppy. It had a hook.

He was such a handsome diver
and his name was Jerry Shine

He kept bopping along behind me, building energy and volume. Suddenly, I realized this was the kind of song that could get stuck in your head for hours. And I was about to spend the next three of them underwater with nothing but the sound of my own bubbles and whatever happened to be running through my head – which I didn't want to be, *I met a handsome diver and his name was Jerry Shine*!

My mask wasn't even on yet but I dropped underwater to escape.

I've just cleared the water from my mask and am on the bottom in front of Ed and Edna's legs. A filefish – two inches long, grayish, and vertically flat – is swimming over the white sand. Its first dorsal fin stands up like a trigger and its tiny mouth is pursed in a perpetual O. It passes over a patch of green seaweed and instantly changes color to match. It changes back just as quickly when it moves over the sand.

Ed and Edna are taking longer than expected to get underwater and I stand up to make sure everything's okay.

"There's a turtle!" someone yells.

A half dozen boys wearing masks dive under. Only their feet are visible, pointing straight up.

I drop under again. An adult hawksbill turtle –

about two feet long, its shell a patchwork of caramels, browns and whites – is lying on the sand while the boys maneuver around it, arms and legs flailing, disposable cameras flashing. I pop back up again.

Ed and Edna are ready. "Let's go straight out to the Snorkel Trail for a few minutes," I say, "then head to the small bridge down on the left."

They nod and the three of us drop under and move out past the turtle and the boys. Within a minute, the boulders of the Snorkel Trail appear. They're teeming with colorful fish – hundreds of them – chromis and puffers and blennies. Ed and Edna settle down on the sand, pointing at different things and filming.

Five minutes pass and they don't move. Not an inch. They're enrapt. After ten minutes, they rise up, move sideways about five feet, then settle back down on the sand, staring into the nooks and crannies and crevices of the boulders, pointing and filming.

The Snorkel Trail is fine but it doesn't compare to the small bridge. I tap Ed on the shoulder and motion to the left in the direction we want to go. Ed nods and the three of us rise up and start swimming. I move past the rest of the boulders and out over the sand. But I have a feeling I'm alone. I turn and look – nothing but empty water.

I swim back and see Ed and Edna on the sand at the end of the boulders, pointing and filming. It takes a few more minutes but I get Ed's attention and motion toward the small bridge. He nods and the three of us head out over the sand again.

As we swim, something big and dark materializes ahead. It's another line of boulders. And as Ed and

Edna sink down in front of it, it suddenly dawns on me why it's called the Snorkel Trail and not the Snorkel Pile of Rocks. There's a 'trail' of them, probably running the entire length of the beach all the way down to the small bridge. And even with a three-hour dive, there might not be enough time for us to get there.

I tap Ed on the shoulder and motion again. He nods and we move out over the sand – until the next line of boulders appears in front of us. I keep swimming past it, hoping they'll follow. But they don't. I swim back and find them on the sand.

Well, Ed and Edna are happy right here. I turn and start toward the bridge by myself. I swim over the same turtle that was being swarmed earlier, now moving along the bottom by itself, taking occasional bites from clumps of seaweed, as if at a salad bar.

Up ahead, the channel cuts to the left. The small bridge is just beyond but I really don't want Ed and Edna to miss it. I swim back. Ed is up in the water column, almost at the surface, filming a moon jelly. Edna is on the sand, staring at something in the boulders.

Ed looks up and I signal for us to surface.

"Let's go to the bridge, Ed. It's right there." I point over to it. "You guys will love it."

Ed nods. "We'll follow you, I promise."

I nod and head back down, deciding not to worry if they don't come. They'll have a great time no matter where they are.

I swim in toward the shore a bit to take us off the line of the Trail and then swim parallel to the beach. A school of mullet – about 300 of them, all a foot long, silver, and built for speed – swims by. The water is only eight feet deep and they fill the water column from the sand to the surface. A smaller school of snappers – larger and deeper-bodied, silver with long yellow stripes – is swimming beside them.

The mullet bend both ways around me, some leaping out of the water above, others skimming the surface, some sifting through the sand, kicking up sediment everywhere. Visibility takes a nose dive.

Within a minute, I reach a small sunken boat that's partially buried. I'm beyond the end of the beach and turn left, passing over huge hermit crabs, fireworms and starfish.

A moment later, the outline of the bridge's supports materializes in front of me, tall and clear and swarming with fish. Schools of French grunts – six inches of alternating blue and yellow stripes – and deep-bodied porgies are streaming up and down and around them. A large scrawled filefish cuts through the water in between the schools. Barracuda are hanging up in the water column, their faces set in Clint Eastwood-like expressions. The largest one, a three-footer, hovers with its mouth agape, razor-sharp teeth exposed with scraps of flesh dangling from them. A group of needlefish hovers near them, within an inch of the surface. They look like the barracuda but are much less muscular. Near the bottom of the closest support, a pair of black and yellow angelfish, each the size of a large dinner plate, moves together, circling each other and the support.

The supports farther in are under the shadow of the bridge and I can barely see them. The water here is deeper, 25 feet. I look back to see if Ed and Edna have followed. They have. Ed's staring wide-eyed.

I move under the bridge into its shadow. It takes a few moments for my eyes to adjust. A pair of divers is poking along the bottom beside me. There's another pair farther ahead. And another up near the surface. There must be 20 other divers under here. A snorkeler is flailing at the surface and then dives under. She's quickly joined by another. There are a dozen of them, too. What a place this is – so much life, so accessible.

I move toward one end of the bridge and the bottom slopes up. The water is only four feet deep and I can see the legs of three snorkelers standing, catching their breath in between dives. Stick-like arrow crabs are scattered across the bottom. So are coral shrimp, puffers and hermit crabs. Within inches of one another, three different species of urchin, each a different color and shape, are tucked into the rocks. There are slate pencil urchins, their bodies a mix of brown, yellow and cream, with thick, widely spaced spines like underwater mines from WWII. There are sea egg urchins, their black bodies almost invisible under short white spines angled in every direction. And there are long spine urchins, with only their black spines sticking out from under ledges.

Grunts are everywhere. Hundreds of them. So are sergeant majors, with thick black and silver vertical bars cut by a horizontal slash of yellow. There are other fish mixed in but it's impossible to pick them all out.

I find the little wreck Markus mentioned. It's dark inside but I angle my lights under the forward deck onto a thicket of spiny lobster antennae so dense I can't see any of the lobsters behind them.

I pass through to the other side of the bridge and sunlight streams down again. It takes a moment for my eyes to re-adjust. There aren't as many divers here. I move along the bottom, past more fireworms and hermit crabs, over mantis shrimp and blennies.

Something weirdly shaped is moving across the bottom. I swim closer and it stops. Its brown body is almost a triangle – a thick triangle, poorly designed for swimming. It's a batfish, with a pair of modified pectoral fins that look like thick, sturdy feet. It has a second pair at the rear of its body that look to have ankles. This fish actually walks on four feet. Its face is set perpetually in a pissed-off expression, coupled with a set of bright red lips. The batfish turns away at a 90-degree angle and walks off.

I rise to the surface and look for Ed's flag. I'm right next to the bridge and there are so many other flags bobbing along that it takes a minute to pick his out. He and Edna are 50 feet away.

I start under again but realize I'm surrounded by big moon jellies, at least 20 of them. It seems as if they're all pulsing toward me. I'm pretty sure they don't have stingers but I'm not going to wait to find out. I drop down to the bottom and back into the shadow of the bridge. When my eyes re-adjust again, I move in close to one of the supports. It's covered with short, brown seaweed. A yellow sea horse – three inches long and holding on by its tail – stands out against it. I move in closer with my light and, as I do, the sea horse gently tucks its head and turns into the weeds.

Ed and Edna are lying on the bottom side-by-side, their faces pressed close to something and don't see me pass. And then I'm back out from under the bridge and into the sunlight again.

I reach the partially buried boat and turn right to head back along the beach. I've been under for two and a half hours and am low on air. But the water is only 12 feet deep so I can stay a while longer.

On the rubble at the stern of the boat, a pair of giant hermit crabs in conch shells are holding onto each other. They look like wrestlers sizing each other up. Suddenly, their claws start windmilling too fast to see. Sand is kicked up all around them in a mini-maelstrom as they throw rapid-fire haymakers at each other. The fight goes on for a minute, then they stop, still holding each other. And then the rapid-fire blows start again.

They fight like this – on again, off again – for five minutes until one of them stretches too far out of its shell and tips over. It rolls onto its back, facing up, struggling to right itself. Finally, it does and slashes back to face the other one but its heart isn't in it anymore. The two back away from each other and disappear.

I turn to head in toward the beach, moving up a slight slope. The bottom turns from rubble to sand. Four yellow heads hover just over it and then disappear. They're garden eels – elusive fish that rise straight up from their holes only when there's absolutely nothing else around. I set down on the sand as flat as I can and stop breathing.

Slowly, all four heads rise up in unison until they're two inches above the bottom, their tails still lodged in their holes. I take a breath and they instantly disappear.

Reluctantly, I pop to the surface. Ed's flag is a short distance away, moving toward me.

The next morning, while I stood in line at the airport waiting to board my flight, I realized I had a song stuck in my head, playing on an endless loop.

> *I met a handsome diver*
> *and his name was Jerry Shine*
> *He was such a handsome diver ...*

The flight back to Boston was a long one.

****

We had reached the doldrums of the dive year. It was almost winter. Life that had migrated in for the summer had now migrated back out. Much of the life that stays was buried or hiding. Even nudibranchs were scarce. By February or March, they would be everywhere. In December, though, most were too small to see.

I pulled into the huge parking lot at Good Harbor Beach in Gloucester – empty except for me – and geared up at my car. Air temps were in the 60s, warmer than expected. I walked on the boardwalk through the grassy dunes to the beach and then crossed the 300 yards of intertidal to the water. Salt Island lay another 200 yards offshore. But with the tide out, the water was shallow enough to walk through all the way to the island's inshore side. When I couldn't walk anymore without going in over my head, I pulled on my fins and went under.

Visibility along the sand/rock interface at the bottom of the island's slope is 30 feet. Sunlight is dancing across the sand. The boulders higher up on the slope are covered with withering blades of kelp, mixed in with the broken stipes of those blades that have already died and been ripped away.

My plan is to circumnavigate the little island, then head in. There are a few crabs about but nothing else.

Seven or eight green metal lobster traps, bent and twisted and tangled with line, are piled up against a boulder. They're no longer buoyed to the surface. They're ghost traps – each one a meaningless menace. A big pollack – heavy-bodied and about two feet long – is trapped inside one, staring out like a bored prisoner. I unhook the bungees holding the trap's door closed and swing it open. The pollock stays inside for the time being. I move along the pile, reaching in to unhook the rest of the doors so nothing else gets caught.

I rise up into the water and look down at the rocky slope and the sand beyond.

There's nothing moving. It looks like a beach town after Labor Day. To dive now, in the doldrums, when there's so little life, you have to find other things to enjoy – the feel of the water, its thick silence, the ability to float free from gravity.

I angle back down through the water, stretching out my arms, dolphin kicking and gliding. Yeah, we're deep in the doldrums. But they won't last long.

****

Two weeks later, I drove back up to Ed's, Christmas music playing the whole way. Joe was driving down from Canada, probably listening to the same thing.

Five hours after leaving my house, Ed, Edna, Joe and I pulled in and parked at a boat launch on Mount Desert Island. The launch looked out over Somes Sound and Acadia National Park. On three sides, the mountains and rocky peaks of the park bounded the dark blue water. The shoreline glistened under a December frost.

"I'm not even bringing a camera," Ed said, holding up a mesh bag. "This is a golf ball site. There's always a ton of them down there."

As sure as I was that Ed didn't play golf, I didn't pursue it. "You're bringing your camera, right, Joe?"

Joe held up his tiny, almost toy camera. "You mean my camera *system*," he said.

White and yellow golf balls are scattered around on the brown muck. I'm only 30 feet from the shore so whoever hit these wasn't very good. Clay skeet targets, pink and intact, are mixed in on the bottom, as well. The water is 42 degrees and visibility is 20 feet. Ed and Joe are swimming straight out, presumably to even better golf ball hunting grounds, and I watch their fins disappear.

I take a hard left along a rock wall that juts up

four feet from the muck. It's covered with sea vases –
white, two inches long and tubular, with pairs of siphons
sucking water in and pumping it out. They're crowded
together by the hundreds, all inhaling and exhaling. Each
is covered with a thin layer of silt. One lone sea peach is
mixed in with them, the last of its kind here, still holding
out for space on the ledge.

I follow the wall until it slopes down into the bottom 50 yards from where it started. Here, a few rocks are
scattered about. I swim straight offshore until, for as far
as I can see, there is nothing but muck. A sand shrimp
sees me and burrows down into it. A green crab does the
same, until only its eyes are visible. I reach down into the
brown silt to see how deep it is and my arm goes in past
the elbow.

I turn around and head back toward the beach,
over the same barren landscape until I near the boat
launch and rocks start to push up. I'm about to surface
but see a large nudibranch colored to blend in with the
muck, lying on its side with a long slime trail – the same
trails left by snails – behind it. It's rolling slightly from
side to side, occasionally lifting up off the bottom and
drifting a bit, anchored by the slime trail, then settling
back down. If it isn't dead, it's very close.

There are no apparent wounds anywhere on
its body and it must have been moving recently – how
else to explain the slime trail. Perhaps it simply died of
old age. That must be rare down here – to live out a full
life before shuffling quietly off this mortal coil. I watch
it twisting and turning in the water for a while, almost
dancing, then head in.

The three of us came out of the water together, just as the sun was setting behind the ridge on the other side of the sound.

"Hold on a second," Edna called. "Let me get a shot of the three of you."

Ed, Joe and I squeezed in together sideways.

"Smile," Edna said, then took what turned out to be the cover photo of this book.

Ed walked back to his truck, whistling and humming, carrying 60 golf balls and a fair number of skeets in his mesh bag. Joe was happy, too. He had pulled up an indestructible dog toy.

We went out to dinner in Bar Harbor, and when we left the restaurant, Joe started dragging his feet. I was going to stay the night and dive with Ed in the morning. But Joe had to head home. After a protracted good-bye, he got in his car and drove off, alone and forlorn. Or as forlorn as Joe can get.

Back at Ed and Edna's, I sat alone on the couch. Big Levi wasn't there. Ed and Edna had had to put him down. I didn't ask about it. I knew that wound was still raw.

Halo, though, sat on the floor beside me. And while Ed and I talked, Nori, their new four-month old Newfie puppy, bounded in and started tearing at my shoe laces. Ed rolled onto the floor laughing and pulled her to him. It looked like he was wrestling a bear cub. He rolled Nori onto her back and she bicycled her hind legs in the air, her puppy teeth happily raking his arms.

"I do all the things you're not supposed to with a puppy," Ed laughed.

Nori twisted to her feet and launched herself onto Ed again. As they wrestled, a parrot behind me took flight from its cage and soared across the room, landing on Edna's shoulder. All was as it should be at Diver Ed's.

The next morning, Ed, Edna, Nori and I pulled into a small cul-de-sac overlooking Otter Cove in Acadia National Park. As at Somes, the downeast beauty of the place was off the charts, with mountains and pine forests and sheer rock cliffs surrounding the water. The wind was blasting, though, and it caught my car door when I opened it, slamming it forward so hard I thought it would rip off.

Edna tied Nori to their truck with a long rope while Ed geared up. A few minutes later, Ed was walking over a field of slippery, soccer ball-sized rocks and into the water.

I, on the other hand, was dawdling. I pulled on one leg of my drysuit, then stared at the water. After a minute, I pulled on the other leg, then stared some more. Then I walked a lap around my car, sat down and stared at the water again. I used to have a buddy – long since deceased – who did this. And the older he got, the more he did it. It drove me crazy.

Now I was doing it. Perhaps age was catching up with me. Finally, I tied my shoes, pulled on the suit the rest of the way and zipped in. I took another lap around my car. As I did, Nori bounded over to me, all black fur and energy. I played with her for a minute, wrestling with her big head until she wrapped her mouth around my leg and punched four or five holes in my drysuit.

I wouldn't be dry on this dive. But I was suddenly energized. I pulled on my tank and picked my way over the rocks into the water. Through the howling wind, I could hear Ed singing, just barely, while cold water trickled in and down my leg.

The bottom is cobble – the same soccer ball-sized rocks as on the beach. The rocks quickly give way to sand, with sunlight streaming down on it. A few small hermit crabs are scurrying about and two whelks are feeding on a dead crab. Other than that, there's not much happening. The doldrums.

I swim straight out from shore to a wall of sea grass, bright green and rising three feet up from the bottom like an unmowed field. The long blades are swaying in the current. A narrow path cuts into the grass, winding left and right and then opening into a small pool of sand. I set down on it and stare into the tall grass circling me. Tiny snails are crawling along on many of the blades. Two juvenile green crabs stare out at me from deeper in, staying motionless.

I take a different path out of the grass and to the sand again. Just as I come out, a school of silver, eel-like fish, 60 to 70 of them, swims by. Each is three inches long and very thin. They're sand lance. Their bodies undulate as if made of rubber. Side-by-side and one atop another, they look like so many silver streamers blowing in the wind.

I follow after them and they change direction as

one. A minute later, they change direction again. They blend in with the water so well that each time they turn, I lose sight of them for a few seconds. When I re-find them, I try to cut them off just a bit. But each time they move a little quicker, undulate a little faster, and keep the distance between us the same.

It's not surprising they're hard to get close to. They're fair game for just about every predator down here, from salmon to whales. The few times in the past that I have managed to get close to them, they've dived head-first into the sand – hence their name. I follow behind this school for as long as I can, falling farther and farther behind, until I peel off and let them go.

Back on the beach, I unzipped my drysuit and pulled it off.

"You're soaked!" Ed yelled. "What happened?"

I looked over at Nori, tail thumping the ground, big doggy smile on her face, a clump of seaweed somehow perched on top of her massive head and just didn't have the heart to tell on her.

"I don't know," I laughed. "I'll figure it out when I get home."

A Bit More Winter

It was early afternoon on New Year's Eve. A few inches of snow covered the ground but the sun was out and warming the day. Except for one pick-up truck parked a few spots ahead of me, I had the beach in Rockport to myself.

I crossed the street and looked out over the sea-wall. The surface of the water was nearly flat but rollers were pulsing through it, breaking on the beach. A mile out, I could see whitecaps slamming into the Sandy Bay Breakwater. An offshore storm was stirring things up. Visibility would not be good. But that didn't matter. I wanted to end the year as I had started it – with a dive right here. And it would be a quick one. I had to get home to celebrate New Year's Eve with Daisy – Chinese takeout and the Stooges.

I started back across the street just as an SUV rounded the corner and came toward me. It was the same make and color as Bobby's and for a split-second I thought it was him. The woman driving it passed by with a wave.

I walked back to my car, suddenly feeling a little

melancholy, and started to gear up. When I was almost done, the truck parked in front of me pulled out onto the road and made a U-turn. It came toward me and slowed to a stop. The driver lowered his window.

"Just so you know, I'm pretty sure you're crazy," he said.

"Yeah, I get that a lot."

"Well, I usually avoid conversations with crazy people," he said, "but, what the hell, Happy New Year."

"You, too," I said.

He turned and looked out at the water. "My grandfather used to dive here. He must have been one of the first."

"Really," I said, slamming my trunk closed. "What was his name?"

He told me but I didn't recognize it. "Yeah, his house was full of portholes and old plates – stuff he pulled off shipwrecks."

Then I saw the man's son, six or seven years old, leaning around him and staring wide-eyed at my camera. "Do you take pictures underwater?" he asked.

"I do," I said.

"Have you ever seen a shark?"

"Have I ever seen a— of course I've seen a shark. What kind of underwater photographer would I be if I had never seen a shark!"

The boy laughed. "What else do you see down there?"

"Aw, come on, he doesn't have time for that," his father said. "He's got to get in the water and we've got to get home."

He turned back to me. "Well, Happy New Year

again. We're going to stay and watch you go in, okay?"

The boy leaned around him even more. "I hope you get some good pictures."

"Thanks," I said. "Happy New Year."

I made my way around the truck, down the ramp to the beach and into the shallows. I took a minute to pull on my mask and fins, then looked up at the truck and waved. When the boy waved back, I dipped under. And the water felt wonderful.

ABOVE: Ed Monat and Edna Martin

BELOW: Connie Bishop and Joe George

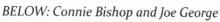

Edna Martin

Andrew Martinez

ABOVE: Bob Boyle, with the author, Daisy Scott and Zeke Shine

BELOW: Andrea Dec

ABOVE: Sandra Edwards, Anne Dupont and Ariane Dimitris

BELOW: the author with Noe Lazo

Martha Lazo

Edna Martin

ABOVE: Ed flexing in front of the Diver Ed Mobile

BELOW: Andy Martinez

Acknowledgments

There are so many people I have to thank for their help while I wrote this book. I could never have done it without the support of the two most important people in my life, my wife Daisy and son Zeke. What they put up with for me to do what I love is never lost on me and I couldn't be more grateful. Thank you, guys.

Many thanks also go to the marine researchers who answered my many questions: Larry Harris of the University of New Hampshire, Daphne Fautin of the University of Kansas, Annie Mercier of Memorial University, Kelly Dorgan of the Dauphin Island Sea Lab, and Kevin Eckelbarger of the University of Maine.

Thanks also to Barbara Gibson, who gave me the use of her wonderful cottage on Lake Winnipesaukee when I needed some time alone to re-focus.

Thanks also to Jonathan Bird for telling me the story of how he first met Gene the Wolffish and the genesis of his name.

Thanks also to everyone I dove with through the year: Joe George, Andrea Dec, Ariane Dimitris, Sandra Edwards, Anne Dupont, Noe Lazo, and Andy Martinez. Special thanks to Ed Monat and Edna Martin, who not only traveled with me on trips to Florida and Quebec but put me up on a couple of occasions.

And while we're on the subject, thanks also to everyone I dove with but who didn't make it into the book. You know who you are and I do, too.

Thanks also to Margaret Estabrook and all the people at United Divers in my hometown of Somerville, Massachusetts, for keeping my tanks filled and my equipment working. I literally could not have done it without you.

I also owe a debt of gratitude to my little guy Romi Gromi, who spent countless hours curled up beside me while I wrote.

Thanks also to my chief graphics enabler, Barbara Hollingdale.

And, finally, a heartfelt thanks to my man Bobby Boyle. Rest in peace, my friend.

Photo Credits

Jerry Shine: the old pier at Eastport, pg 27; Folly Cove, pg 48; Pierce Island parking lot, pg 58; Manasquan Jetty, pg 68; the Blue Heron Bridge, pg 100; Old Sow, pg 121; torpedo bottle, 138; Jasper Beach, pg 141; Rockport at night, pg 155; Ed Monat and Edna Martin, pg 171; Andrea Dec, Sandra Edwards, Anne Dupont, Ariane Dimitris, pg172; Andy Martinez, pg 173; the quay in the Saguenay, pg 185; Dolibers Cove, pg 195; the small bridge at the Blue Heron, pg 204; three anemones, Gene the wolffish, and a nudibranch, back cover.
All photos © Jerry Shine

Edna Martin: Ed Monat, Joe George, Jerry Shine, front cover; Connie Bishop, Joe George, pg 171; Ed Monat and the Diver Ed Mobile, pg 173; Ed Monat at Escoumins, pg 182; Jerry Shine at Escoumins, back cover.
All photos © Edna Martin

Andrew Martinez: Bob Boyle, Jerry Shine; Daisy Scott, Zeke Shine, pg 171
© Andrew Martinez

Daisy Scott: Jerry Shine bio photos, pg 237 and back cover
© Daisy Scott

Martha Lazo: Jerry Shine, Noe Lazo, pg 172
© Martha Lazo

For More Photos

Jerry Shine regularly posts underwater and surface photos on his webpage, www.jerryshine.com, and on his Facebook page, Jerry Shine Photography. To see the creatures described in this book, as well as many others, check those sites.

About the Author

Jerry Shine's been looking at the water and wondering what's happening beneath it for as long as he can remember. He was certified to dive at 14, began diving in earnest in college and hasn't looked back since. There's still nothing he loves as much as spending time on, near, or under the water with family and friends, and he hopes to keep doing so well into his hundreds.